Built-in Furniture

Built-in Furniture

Jim Tolpin

The Taunton Press

The Taunton Press
Inspiration for hands-on living™

©2002 by The Taunton Press, Inc.

Printed in the United States of America
10 9 8 7 6 5 4 3

Built-In Furniture was originally published in hardcover
in 1997 by The Taunton Press, Inc.

The Taunton Press, 63 South Main Street, PO Box 5506,
Newtown, CT 06470-5506
e-mail: tp@taunton.com

Distributed by Publishers Group West

Library of Congress Cataloging-in-Publication Data
Tolpin, Jim, 1947-
    Built-in furniture / Jim Tolpin.
      p.   cm.
    "A Fine woodworking book."
    Includes index.
    ISBN 1-56158-121-6 hardcover
    ISBN 1-56158-395-2 paperback with flaps
    ISBN 1-56158-637-4 paperback
1. Built-in furniture. 2. Cabinetwork. I. Title.
    TT197.5.B8T65   1997   96-44421
    684.1'6 — dc21   CIP

To Laura Tringali.

This writing business has been a long, sometimes tough, but always rewarding road—
I'm eternally grateful that you were there at the starting gate.

ACKNOWLEDGMENTS

As always, there are many people to thank for the inspirations and contributions that helped bring this book to reality. At The Taunton Press, Jim Chiavelli and Helen Albert got this project off the ground while Rick Peters, Joanne Renna, Ruth Dobsevage, and Chris Casey kept it going. Craig Savage helped track down craftsmen in the Santa Barbara, California, area, finding people who would make an immense contribution to this book. Long-time friend Nat Natali took time away from designing satellite positioning systems to help with the shelf sag graph. Friend and go-getter Michele Bruns got on the phone to track down the people behind some of the projects. Photographers Craig Wester and Sandor Nagyszalanczy, though burdened by my backseat driving, pulled off some difficult photo shoots. Catherine Parkman lent her loving support throughout the creation of this book, easing the truly daunting task of compiling so much good work from so many people. Which brings me to my final, most grateful acknowledgment: all the contributors to this book—architects, builders, and hobbyists, who all took the time, some of it considerable, to help me elucidate their work.

Recessed shelving designed by architect Jonathan Livingston, of San Francisco, Calif., lends a spacious feeling to this kitchen. Photo by Charles Miller.

Continuous built-in desks and storage cabinets wrap the perimeter
of this home office, designed by Jefferson Riley, of Centerbrook
Architects, Essex, Conn., and built by Russ Alger and Don Hills.
Photo © Brian Vanden Brink.

CONTENTS

INTRODUCTION

"It is quite impossible to consider the building as one thing and its furnishings another...the very chairs, tables and cabinets—where practical—are of the building, never fixtures upon it."

— Frank Lloyd Wright,
American Architecture

I'd wager that you could find built-in furniture in nearly any type of American home: from the parlor-wall storage cupboards of the earliest New England saltboxes to the family-room/audiovisual entertainment centers of the neo-modern villas lining California's Skyline Boulevard. Why are built-ins so ubiquitous in our homes?

For the early colonists, storage and comfort were important needs. Built-in cupboards provided the most storage space for the lowest cost and maximized the use of the interior space of the thick, timber-framed walls. Other built-in furnishings were created to satisfy the need for comfort: Benches worked into an alcove by the fireplace created a warm, cozy space within these notoriously chilly homes.

For later American designers and builders—notably Frank Lloyd Wright and Greene and Greene—architectural unity was the goal. Built-in furnishings allowed these designers unprecedented control over the ultimate look and function of the home. Rather than having to work around existing free-standing furniture, they would, with built-in furnishings, design interior spaces that achieved a unique, yet comfortable, effect: an interior landscape in which highly functional furnishings blended harmoniously into their surroundings.

Because the creation of built-in furnishings often demands unique design, construction, and installation techniques, this book begins with chapters devoted to these issues. Armed with some fundamental principles, you then embark on a room-by-room inspection of contemporary built-ins chosen for their visual appeal, unique design solutions, or extraordinary detailing. It is a close look that includes detailed explanations and illustrations of the special design, construction, and installation strategies used by their builders. By the end of this book, I'm sure you will agree with me that built-in furnishings are far more than "furniture without legs."

Storybook-like built-in beds make memorable sleeping spaces in a turn-of-the-century island retreat. Designer and builder unknown. Photo © Brian Vanden Brink.

Cupboards were built in around the parlor fireplace in the 1651 home of Tristram Coffin in Newbury, Mass. Courtesy The Society for The Preservation of New England Antiquities.

1

ARCHITECTURAL

FURNITURE

Deeply rooted in the Old World, from the ornate vestry furnishings of the church to the humble chimney cupboards of the peasant cottage, built-ins have been with us in our shelters for many centuries. From grandiose to downright secretive, these fascinating furnishings have been the understory of story tales—and the functional companions of our everyday lives.

Colonial Built-in Cabinetry

Furniture without legs—"architectural furniture" that owes at least some of its existence to the interior structure of the building—appeared in some of the earliest homes raised in the infant American colonies. These furnishings were not luxuries—they may in fact have contributed to the survival of these first Americans. For most new settlers, stand-alone furniture to contain food stores and eating implements was scarce, and few could afford to bring their furniture with them to the New World—assuming they owned any to begin with. In those tenuous early days, time was scarce as well. Considering the uncertainties of living among wary Indians and the early onset of the New England winter, it was well for a new settler to get into a livable structure as soon as possible.

Because built-in furnishings could use the house structure for their back, sides, floor, and ceiling, they were significantly easier—and thus faster—to build than the stand-alone furniture of this era, which often featured sculpted legs and carved moldings. Most house carpenters could, and would, create storage cupboards and shelving while immersed in the construction of the house itself. Indeed, the walls of these homes, which were composed of timbers 8 in. or more in depth, practically begged for built-ins to take advantage of the space between posts.

By the 18th century (when things were starting to settle down a bit), colonial craftsman were expending their best efforts on these built-in furnishings. Some examples, as epitomized by the cabinet in the photo at left, would equal in style and execution the finest stand-

A typical Colonial-era china hutch. Photo © Brian Vanden Brink.

alone furniture of the day. Corner china cupboards, embellished with a dramatic hand-carved cockleshell-type molding, pushed these woodworkers' talents to the limit. Other built-in pieces featured doors with delicately molded, curved sash and used complex moldings to integrate them into the rest of the room's woodwork. These fine architectural furnishings added much civility and elegance to the relatively simple homes of early America.

Architectural Furniture of the Shakers

While stand-alone Shaker furniture has achieved worldwide renown, a visit to any of their museum communities reveals another, though lesser-known, treasure: built-in furnishings. From tiny cupboards recessed into dining-room walls to sweeping attic storage cupboards and drawers (see the photo below), this architectural furniture also sheds light on why the Shakers built as they did.

Appearing in the late 18th and early 19th centuries, the architectural furniture of Shaker-made buildings was far more ubiquitous than the built-ins that appeared in Colonial through Federal period homes of the "outside" world. While for most early Americans built-ins satisfied the need for function and economy, for the Shakers these furnishings satisfied the tenets of their creed, particularly their profound quest for simplicity, precise function, and lack of adornment. (There was no need for a Shaker designer to worry about the design of legs or of moldings to run along

Attic storage cabinets (probably for bedding, winter coats, and other out-of-season clothing) at the Canterbury, N. H., Shaker community. Photo by Tim Rieman.

top edges or side corners—these borders generally found resolution through their integration with the room trim.) Another particularly desirable and inherent attribute of built-ins—their cleanliness—also appealed to Shaker sensibilities. Because most of these furnishings were recessed into walls, there were few exposed horizontal surfaces or hollow places in which dust could accumulate.

Gustav Stickley's Structural Furnishings

Gustav Stickley, the widely regarded father of the Craftsman movement in America in the late 19th century, clearly articulated the importance of built-ins in home architecture, calling them "an essential part of the Craftsman idea."

Reasoning that a person's house should not present a different "scheme of attractiveness" than its furnishings, Stickley insisted that when a builder leaves a house it should be ready to live in—"a place that holds its own welcome forever," not "a barren uninviting prison-like spot [requiring] furniture and walls hidden under pictures." He designed the furnishings as essential structural features of the house, judiciously making

In this living room/library/office designed by Gustav Stickley, wall-spanning shelving and cupboards surround a built-in pigeonhole desk. Note the built-in window seat. Courtesy Dover Publications.

use of the rest of the woodwork (trim) to augment the built-ins and blend them in with the overall scheme of the home.

Throughout Stickley's career, built-ins were a cornerstone of his interior architecture. His kitchens (an example is shown in the illustration above) were among the first to feature extensive built-in cupboards and drawers to provide "a place for everything and everything in its place." Like the Shakers, Stickley also reasoned that cabinetry with no gaps between the floor or ceiling would make a room—in this case a kitchen—much easier to keep clean.

In his dining rooms, Stickley often designed a wall alcove to contain a built-in sideboard and china cupboards. This not only increased the open space of these typically small rooms, but added much beauty and charm. In the illustration at right, note his careful attention to molding details—the wainscot height appears to define the proportions of the cupboard as well as the height of the alcove windows.

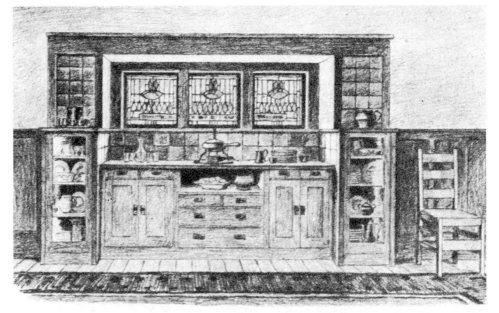

A Stickley sideboard and china cupboards built into an alcove off a dining room. Windows, tiles, and side cupboards all align with the top of the wainscot. Courtesy Dover Publications.

The Interior Architecture of Frank Lloyd Wright

Expanding on the Craftsman idea that built-in furnishings could enhance the architecture of a home, Frank Lloyd Wright realized that furniture could, when given the attention it deserves, be the architecture of an interior space. In his own words: "The interior space [and thus its furnishings] is the reality of the building...the room must be seen as architecture or we have no architecture." For this architect, furniture was to be "of the building, not fixtures imposed upon it."

Emboldened by this concept, Wright used built-in furnishings to liberate the rooms within his houses, creating expansive, well-lighted spaces in which the traditional boundaries and junctures of wall, ceiling, and floor ceased to dictate the design. He often specified large-scale, complex furnishings that could not only provide seating and bookshelves, but also contain lighting and heat ductwork (see the photo below for an example). Wright's built-ins defined the interior architecture of a building in an entirely new way. Now a large furnishing could be used in place of a wall to give boundaries to a space and fulfill a multitude of functions at one time. Some built-ins, such as the window seat seen in the photo on the facing page, create a dramatic effect that lends grandeur as well as function to the room.

Library shelving/seating in Frank Lloyd Wright's Meyer Mayhouse in Grand Rapids, Mich., creates a wall, delineating the living room without sequestering it from the rest of the house. The latticework above the shelving lets light and air through, matching the unit projecting from the opposite wall. Photo by Jon Miller © Hedrich Blessing.

A combination window seat/alcove makes a dramatic statement in Frank Lloyd Wright's large family room. Large storage drawers take advantage of the space created by the raised alcove platform. Photo by Jon Miller © Hedrich Blessing.

Built-ins in Contemporary Architecture

Large, multipurpose rooms are one of the hallmarks of contemporary American homes, and well-designed built-ins are a good way to make that space more functional without losing its open feeling.

BUILT-INS AS ROOM DIVIDERS

When architect Ed Weinstein, of Seattle, Washington, set out to design his own residence, he decided to endow the rooms liberally with built-ins. These furnishings would define and make a versatile, appealing space for his active— and interactive—family. His design philosophy builds upon that of Stickley and Wright: "Because built-in cabinetry is the interior architecture, it is, in fact, the home. When you come into a house with extensive built-ins, you feel immediately welcomed...you have entered a home." In the great room shown in the photo on p. 12, Weinstein combined the kitchen with the living area using built-in furniture to lend definition and a multitude of functions to the broad, open space.

A room divider in Ed Weinstein's home separates the kitchen from the rest of the great room. Photo by Craig Wester.

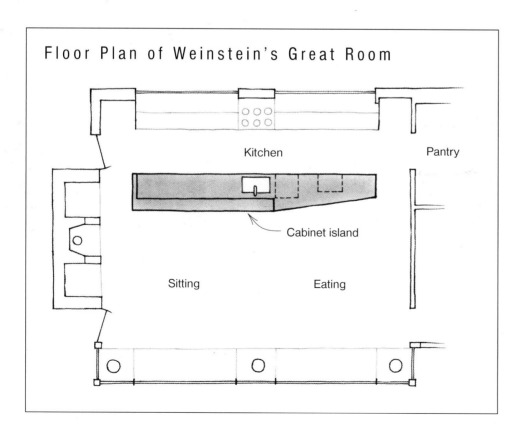

Floor Plan of Weinstein's Great Room

Kitchen

Pantry

Cabinet island

Sitting

Eating

When you enter the great room, the first thing you may notice is a massive island of cabinets running almost the entire length of the room. This architectural furnishing, built by Bill Walker, of Seattle, Washington, provides kitchen storage on one side and book shelving (toward the living-room area) on the other. Its primary function is to separate—without isolating—the corridor-style kitchen from the living area. Notice the low box fixed to the stainless-steel countertop. Designed to contain cookbooks, some appliances, and hand towels, it also functions to block the view of these items as well as the sink (with its inevitable dirty dishes) from the living area. You can still, however, see across the top of the island and through the windows set between the upper and lower kitchen cabinets on the far side wall. Weinstein's living area,

An inglenook off the sitting room of Stickley's Craftsman cottage No. 93. Courtesy Dover Publications.

filled with views to the outside and plenty of natural light from all directions, gives you a feeling of great expanse without sacrificing a sense of coziness. Built-ins are major contributors to this uniquely comfortable and functional roomscape.

BUILT-INS AS MINI-ENVIRONMENTS

One of the earliest reasons for the creation of built-in furnishings may have been to create a mini-environment within a larger room. A good example of this is the fireplace inglenook, shown in the illustration above as interpreted in a Craftsman-era cottage. Here one could have warmth and intimacy, yet not feel completely isolated from the rest of the home and family.

In more contemporary interpretations, architects have expanded upon the age-old concept of the inglenook, using extensive built-ins to create an entire reading room or sitting room. For example, in the living room shown in the photo at right, architect Geoffrey Prentiss, of Seattle, Washington, used a centrally located woodstove, flanking

Geoffrey Prentiss's raised alcove is a modern interpretation of the inglenook. Photo by Craig Wester.

bookshelves and a raised platform to differentiate the alcove, built by Peter Kilpatrick, of Friday Harbor, Washington, from the rest of the living room. Comfortable couch/daybeds with large drawers for bedding and guest linens line opposite walls. Note how the generous proportions of the cubicles formed by the adjustable shelves give the entire room—which is really quite small—a sense of spaciousness.

In the work shown in the photo at left, Jefferson Riley, of Centerbrook Architects, Essex, Connecticut, has taken the inglenook concept a step further, creating a sitting room/guest bedroom in an alcove that projects over an open living space. Built-in benches line the perimeter of the alcove and double as guest beds—the drawers on the facing below the cushions contain bedding. The project was built by Yoder and Sons, of Middlefield, Ohio.

The *engawa,* one of the hallmarks of Japanese architecture, is a transitional space set along the edge of a living area. Its purpose is to soften the distinction between the inside of the house and the outside garden. Len Brackett, of Nevada City, California, modified the Japanese-style *engawa* to Western use by raising it up from floor level about 16 in., creating a raised sitting or sleeping space (with bedding storage below). The primary reason he raised the *engawa* was to make it work with Western-style furniture inside the house. "I felt it was necessary to make sure the eye levels of people sitting on furniture and those sitting in the *engawa* are equal. This is one of the keys to adapting traditional Japanese architecture to Western styles of living (where furniture is used)."

Entering the space, you orient yourself to either the outside or the inside of the house, depending on which sliding door you open or close. By leaving both doors open (see the photo at left),

Above: A room within a room, the sitting room/guest bedroom by Jefferson Riley perches on posts over the living room. Photo © Brian Vanden Brink.

Right: A Westernized version of the Japanese *engawa*, by Len Brackett, eases the transition between the interior of the house and the outdoors. Photo by Jeffrey Westman.

A curved wall-to-wall unit by D. Ralph Katz includes a fireplace surround, display shelving, and a home theater. Photo by Blanchard Photography.

you can draw the garden into the house. Like the traditional inglenook and the more contemporary alcove-style seating, an *engawa* creates a mini-environment that not only gives definition and function to the interior architecture of a space, but also can actually become a space in its own right.

BUILT-INS ON THE CUTTING EDGE

In addition to being asked by contemporary architects to redefine our interior living spaces, a modern built-in may also be asked to serve some functions unheard of as recently as 25 years ago. For example, consider the ultra-sleek wall unit designed by D. Ralph Katz, of Cranbury, New Jersey, and shown in the photo above. Sweeping fully across one side of a living room, it contains within its graceful curves not only the traditional fireplace and hearth, but also a home-theater entertainment center complete with electronic controls, a speaker system and sound equipment, open display shelving for artwork, and extensive storage cupboards. The unit was built by Timberline Cabinets, also of Cranbury.

Clearly, built-in furnishings have come a long way from their roots in the traditional wall cupboards of Colonial-era America, yet still their basic purpose remains the same: to lend beauty, function, and economy to an interior space.

Massive in scale and presence, this 12-ft.-high by 20-ft.-long shelving unit by Richard Wedler stands in the library of St. John's Seminary in Camarillo, Calif. Photo by Richard Wedler.

2
DESIGNING BUILT-INS

It may be that built-ins put more demands on their designers and builders than freestanding furniture. A large built-in can require a major outlay of time and materials. But more important, the design elements and construction methods must be right the first time out. Once in place, a built-in commits a space to a specific use—a change or removal could be a nightmare for both the cabinetmaker and the homeowner.

But a thoughtfully designed and soundly constructed built-in furnishing is well worth the effort. No other piece of furniture can be shaped, textured, or painted to enhance or to blend in seamlessly with a particular architectural style. Built-ins can be built specifically to accommodate certain objects; they can be configured to make the best use of an unusual space (or to create a space within a space,

A wet bar and storage cupboards by Richard Wedler blend seamlessly into the interior of a California home. Note the pass-through to the kitchen, the space-saving recessed shelving in the wall around the window, and the dramatic mahogany bartop. Photo by Richard Wedler.

Brian Weerts's art-furniture Avonite and aluminum credenza flanked by sweeping arches of brass-faced display shelving has a commanding presence in this otherwise traditionally styled living room. Photo by Brian Weerts.

as seen in Chapter 1); and they can be designed to make a minimal demand on floor space. And because built-ins can often make use of existing surfaces as floors, ceilings, and sidewalls, they often use less material than freestanding furniture of the same volume.

Designing for Style

In most cases, designers plan a built-in furnishing to complement the interior decor and to blend seamlessly at its boundaries with the existing architecture of the home. One of the more endearing aspects of a well-executed built-in is, in fact, its ability to look as if it has always been there. Unlike freestanding furnishings, a built-in is rarely added on a whim to a room. Instead, most architectural furniture is designed with the idea of not conflicting with other design elements within the room.

This design approach is exemplified by the wet bar and dining-room cabinetry designed and built by Richard Wedler, of North Hollywood, California, and shown in the photo above left. By custom-cutting shaper knives from blank tool steel, Wedler was able to match the moldings on the built-in work to the moldings already in the room. The overall design—white surfaces, raised panel doors, brass pulls, exposed butt hinges, and the arched opening over the wet-bar alcove—reflect the period styling and millwork in the rest of the home.

It is also possible to break with convention to allow a built-in to make an impressive, visually exciting statement—to create its own context within its surroundings. While the credenza and display shelving designed and built by Brian Weerts, of St. Anne, Illinois, does take some of its inspiration from a traditional-style arched window in the room (see the photo at left), its sweeping curves of decidedly non-traditional materials (black aluminum, sheet brass, and Avonite) make a dramatic contribution to the room. Yet it does not, at least to my eye, create a jarring non sequitur. More massive than most stand-alone furniture pieces, this built-in makes a powerful design statement that transforms the interior architecture of this room—something I'd wager a smaller furniture piece of noncongruous design might not be powerful enough to pull off.

In some instances, especially where the built-in furnishings dominate an entire room, built-ins can offer the opportunity to express a style unique to that room, effectively becoming the interior architecture of the space. When cabinetmaker Ross Day, of Seattle, Washington, sat down with his clients to discuss the remodel of their master bedroom, he was asked to create a room with a "contemporary Asian" feeling. The furnishings to be built, which are shown in the floor-plan drawing at right, included three wardrobe units, two bookcases, a corner cabinet, an entertainment/display center, three sliding screens, a platform bed with storage drawers, and two nightstands—more than enough palette on which to express this design imperative.

To anchor the pieces in an Asian-like motif, Day repeated a simple latticework pattern on the door faces of each unit (see the photo above right), including *shoji*-style doors on the nightstands. The choice of wood—clear, vertical-grain oak—and exposed "Chinese puzzle" proud joinery on the counter edges further support the Oriental imagery.

The distinctive styling of this oak bedroom suite by Ross Day firmly establishes and defines the interior landscape of the room. Photo by Mike Seidl.

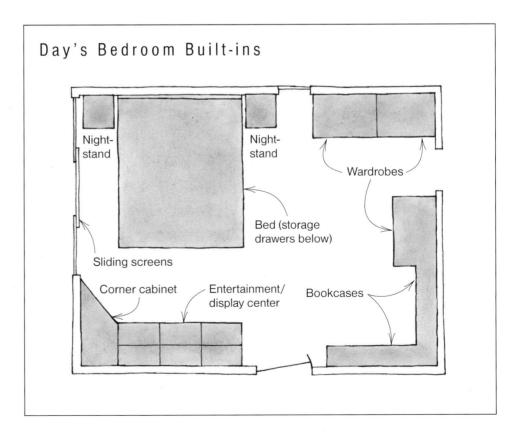

Day's Bedroom Built-ins

Nightstand

Nightstand

Wardrobes

Bed (storage drawers below)

Sliding screens

Corner cabinet

Entertainment/ display center

Bookcases

Designing for Function

Of course, style isn't everything—you must also be sure when designing a piece of built-in furniture that it works well for its intended purpose. For example, the art display alcove designed and built by South Mountain Co., of Chilmark, Massachusetts, and shown in the photo at left is a successful piece because of its pleasing proportions and tasteful restraint in the use of wood trim. The unusual light fixture adds to the effect through its shape (which complements the vase) and through the split-lighting effect that sends a strong light up to the ceiling for general illumination and a more subdued direct light toward the art object cradled in the alcove.

A more utilitarian built-in is the box designed by the homeowner with builder Bill Walker, of Seattle, Washington, for the entryway of a house by the water. The low box, which is shown in the photo below, serves first as a seat: Children covered with sand from the beach can sit on the box while removing their shoes. When the lid of the box is lifted, two more functions

South Mountain's wall alcove, in combination with a custom-made light fixture, tastefully and effectively showcases a vase. Photo by Derrill Bazzy.

Though simple in form and style, this entryway box by Bill Walker serves a multitude of functions: seat, shoe box, and laundry chute. Photo by Craig Wester.

reveal themselves. On one side, a compartment accepts wet beach shoes; on the other, a laundry chute transports dirty outerwear quickly and cleanly to the basement.

Another example of a built-in furnishing that performs a multitude of functions is the combination kitchen work-station/entertainment center designed by architect Albert Pastine, of San Francisco, California, and shown in the photos at right. The portion of the unit facing the kitchen provides extensive storage behind cupboard doors, pot and pan storage in oversized drawers, and an ample work surface. The side facing the family room contains audiovisual equipment and media ware. Recessed lighting in the ceiling provides direct illumination to both faces of the unit, while hidden up-lighting in the built-in's soffit diffuses the lighting to the rest of the room. The piece was built by Alex Pastine and Carl Johnson.

When designing a furnishing of this scale, it is imperative to consider the impact it will have on the look and function of the space around it—which in this case includes an adjoining room. To be sure the furnishing will function properly, try to visualize it in place. It may prove helpful to build a full-scale cardboard mockup and set it in place on site. In this way, you can see clearly how the unit affects the traffic patterns through the room. You may discover that the unit draws people right in front of a passage or closet door, or that it interferes with access to another furnishing. The new built-in may also require some adjustment in room lighting, both to illuminate the unit itself and to adjust for any interference it may cause to existing lighting (both natural and electric).

Centrally placed between the kitchen and family room, this double-duty furnishing designed by Albert Pastine serves as a kitchen cupboard and work surface on one side (left) and an audiovisual cabinet on the other. Photo at left by Albert Pastine; photo below © Douglas A. Salin.

Sometimes the function of a built-in furnishing is not what it might first appear. Consider, for example, the corner cupboard/bookshelf shown in the photos at left. Not only is the cupboard fake, but so are the books—designer and builder Ronald Saulnier, of Bayville, New York, created them with acrylic paints. This "built-in" is in reality a door—a solution to a remodeling problem that called for bathroom access in the same place where the homeowner wanted to keep an original corner cupboard. To camouflage the door, Saulnier carefully designed the moldings to appear continuous when the door is closed. The use of bead molding around the door itself and hidden hinges contribute to the illusion.

Designing for Economy

This last principle guiding the design of built-ins—economy—refers to what built-ins do best: make the most of limited space. As you will see in the examples that follow and then throughout the rest of this book, designers can call for built-ins for nearly any nook or cranny in a house. It seems the smaller the home, the more this principle comes into play—a tiny apartment can boast more functional storage spaces than a house nearly twice its size.

Ronald Saulnier's unit (above) looks like a built-in corner cupboard for books. But as you can see at right, this is but an illusion—it is simply a door to a bathroom. Photos by Rob Rich.

Stairways present an unusually challenging, though promising, opportunity for the designer of built-ins. This triangular space, wasted in most homes, can be used for storage. Designer and builder John Hermannsson, of Redwood City, California, installed a pull-out shoe bin under a stair (see the photo at right). When closed, the bin is hidden behind a wall panel.

Architect Ross Chapin, of Langley, Washington, filled the space under a set of stairs with a plethora of drawers and cupboards, providing much-needed storage in a home with a limited floor plan. Notice in the photo below how he recessed the face of the built-ins under the stairway—though this reduces the overall depth of the units, it actually helps to improve access—deep storage spaces tend to get cluttered at the front, making it difficult to reach toward the back of the space. In the resulting overhang, he installed a recessed lighting fixture that illuminates the storage-space interiors.

John Hermannsson's shoe bin slides out on full-extension drawer hardware from underneath a stair. Photo by John Hermannsson.

Drawers and cupboards by Ross Chapin fill the space under a stairway, making full use of this odd-shaped space. Photo by Ross Chapin.

Bookshelves follow these stairs up from the living room to the bedrooms in John Parker's unusual but highly efficient use of space. Photo by Sloan T. Howard Photography.

24 CHAPTER TWO

At first thought, a stairway would seem an inappropriate place to locate a bookshelf. But in this case it made sense to architect John Parker, of Glastonbury, Connecticut, to make the stairway a visual and functional extension of the living room/library where it originates (see the photo on the facing page). What more encouragement would you need to grab a book on your way up to bed? It's a surprisingly effective and attractive solution.

Architect Andy Neumann, of Carpinteria, California, took advantage of a large stairway landing to create a small office, which is shown in the top photo at right. Though the level of the landing changes by several steps, it did not hinder the design. Instead, it created an opportunity for stepping the cabinets up the stairs and adding another desk for a computer station. A built-in couch gives the area a sense of coziness and companionship, not to mention a place to rest between bouts of paperwork. These stair-landing built-ins, which were built by Doug Ford, effectively add a room to the house.

Stairways aren't the only areas within a home that can benefit from designing for economy of space. Cliff Nathan, of Studio City, California, was given the challenge of creating cupboards for china in a tiny (less than 4 sq. ft.) space angled between a refrigerator and the end of a kitchen wall. His solution, shown in the bottom photo at right, was simple and effective: He filled the angle from corner to corner with upper and lower case cabinetry. To provide easy access to the interior of the units from either the kitchen or the dining area, he hinged the paired doors to a middle partition.

Above: Andy Neumann created an open but cozy office space by designing built-in furnishings for a stair landing. Photo by Bill Zeldis.

Left: Cliff Nathan's simple base and upper cabinets make the most of a transition area between a refrigerator and a wall. Photo by Cliff Nathan.

This ash wood couch (which pulls out into a daybed) and its surrounding furnishings fill the attic of Scott Wynn's home. Photo by Scott Wynn.

The attic is another area that can offer tremendous opportunities for the designer of built-in furnishings. In one attic remodel project, architect/builder Scott Wynn, of San Francisco, California, filled the space under the roof eaves with a feast of built-ins. Along one side Wynn created an office area complete with a computer desk, extensive shelving and large lateral-file drawers. The bottom file drawer, which is 40 in. deep, takes full advantage of the available area in the space created by the angled roof line. The oversized drawer rides on furniture casters to ease access, while the drawers above slide out on full-extension, side-mount drawer slides.

On the opposite wall Wynn built in a couch/daybed (see the photo above), with a bank of drawers on both sides.

More shelving and several 4-ft.-high closets behind cabinet-style doors complete the remodel.

Sometimes a built-in must provide nearly all the storage for a tiny residence. Faced with that problem, architect Rick A. Share, of New York City, designed a sweeping wall unit, shown in the top photo on the facing page, for an 800-sq.-ft. one-bedroom penthouse apartment. Behind a visually rich mosaic of paneled doors and drawer faces, the wall unit, which was built in solid cherry and cherry plywoods by Gene Shaw, of Lancaster, Pennsylvania, contains a built-in desk system (see the bottom photo on the facing page), file drawers, blanket drawers, three hanging closets, a "recreation department" (a storage cupboard with hanging systems for

Rick A. Share's wall system fills the entire side wall of a New York City apartment. Not surprisingly, it provides for nearly all the storage needs of the space. A desk (left) snuggles into one section of the wall. Photos by Whitney Cox.

Peter Albrecht's entertainment center, built of clear vertical-grain fir, is illuminated inside and out by inset incandescent lighting on dimmer switches. Photo by Craig Wester.

Halogen strip lighting, set into the cornice of library shelving by Neil K. Johnson, floods the spines of the books, making book selection easy on the eyes. Photo by Neil K. Johnson.

sports gear), entertainment equipment, and an assortment of adjustable-shelf storage cupboards in various shapes. Because the unit so effectively economizes on the available space, it eliminated the need for bedroom and utility closets. This, in turn, maximized the amount of open space—a premium commodity in such a small apartment.

Lighting Systems for Built-in Furnishings

The lighting of a built-in furnishing is an element of design that should not be ignored—without its careful consideration the piece may not achieve its full aesthetic and functional potential. In the entertainment center shown in the photo on the facing page, incandescent lights set into the ceiling provide down-lighting to its interior shelves, focusing attention on the art objects displayed

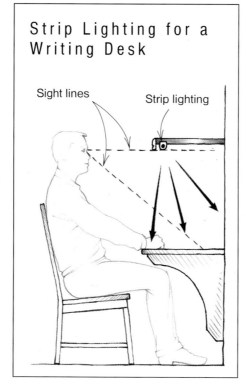

Strip Lighting for a Writing Desk

Sight lines

Strip lighting

there. Because the furnishing itself obviously deserves attention, the designer and builder, Peter Albrecht, of Port Townsend, Washington, installed swiveling task lighting into the ceiling in front of the unit to bathe the face in a rich, warm light, bringing out the full beauty of the wood.

Downlighting is much appreciated with bookshelves, especially if it serves to illuminate the spines of the books to make their titles easy to read. In the shelving shown in the photo on p. 29, a halogen light strip set into the slight overhang behind a cornice molding washes light across the entire face of the unit. This placement is ideal—freestanding floor lamps or lights set in the ceiling in front of the shelves tend to cast shadows when one stands in front of the books. The shelving was designed by Neil K. Johnson, of Cinnaminson, New Jersey, and built by Mark C. Rombach.

The drawing above left shows a subtle way to provide ample light to a writing desk. A lighting strip placed in a groove and behind an edge molding is invisible and free of glare.

In the built-in shown in the photo at left, downlighting from elegant low-voltage brass-ringed canister lights illuminates the interior of a china cabinet. (For more on low-voltage lighting, see the sidebar on the facing page.) The lights are only $5/8$ in. deep and set into a hole bored into the case stock. Glass shelves allow light to pass through to lower shelves. The cabinet was designed by architect Louis Mackall, of Guilford, Connecticut, and built by Breakfast Woodworks, also of Guilford.

Downlighting from elegant low-voltage brass-ringed canister lights illuminates the interior of a china cabinet by Louis Mackall. Glass shelving allows light to pass through to the lower levels. Photo © Karen Bussolini.

LOW-VOLTAGE LIGHTING

A Typical Low-voltage System

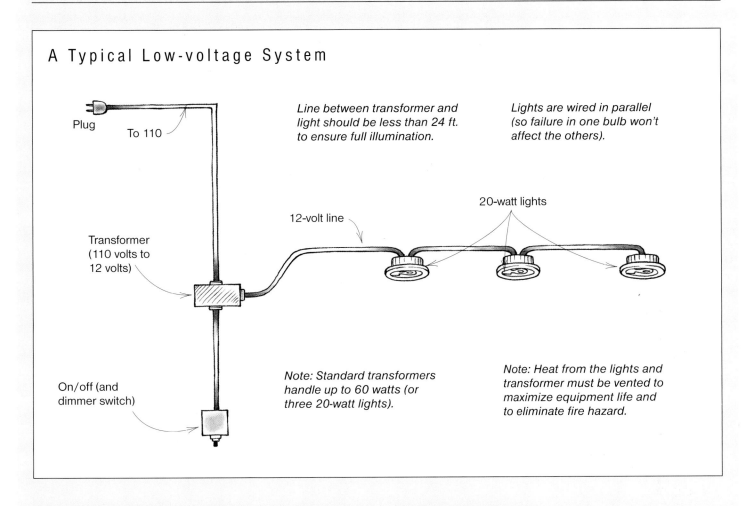

Plug

To 110

Line between transformer and light should be less than 24 ft. to ensure full illumination.

Lights are wired in parallel (so failure in one bulb won't affect the others).

20-watt lights

12-volt line

Transformer (110 volts to 12 volts)

On/off (and dimmer switch)

Note: Standard transformers handle up to 60 watts (or three 20-watt lights).

Note: Heat from the lights and transformer must be vented to maximize equipment life and to eliminate fire hazard.

Twelve-volt lighting systems are ideal for lighting built-in furnishings. They are small in size, yet offer ample illumination with a pleasing natural light. Because these lights need only half the wattage of an incandescent lamp to provide the same amount of illumination, low-voltage lighting systems can be smaller, run cooler, and typically last nearly twice as long. Because of the low voltage, the wires are much smaller and easier to run (and safer) than wires for a 110-volt system.

The halogen lamps these systems use can provide a general wash lighting (typically with a series of 20-watt fixtures), or highly effective task lighting at higher wattages. Switches range from standard flip or dimmer switches to touch switches wired to a pull knob or hinge (multiple touches increase the illumination in one type of dimmer switch), to a microswitch that rests against a door (the light goes on when you open the door).

Classic design elements executed with standard modern furniture-making techniques lend an elegant, traditional "English" look to Stephen Cabitt's reading-room addition. Photo by Dean Powell.

3
PRINCIPLES OF BUILT-IN
CONSTRUCTION

Constructing a typical built-in furnishing involves many of the same processes as building a stand-alone piece of furniture of similar function. The assembly of the doors, drawers, shelving, and usually the face frame is identical. Sometimes, however, the case components of a built-in may be radically different from those of a stand-alone piece of furniture. It's not uncommon for there to be no internal casework at all—the structure of the building may provide the floor, back, sides, and ceiling of the built-in. Because nearly any type of built-in unit gets some, if not all, of its dimensional stability from the structure (and because it need never be moved), the construction elements that provide strength to a movable piece of furniture (such as mortise-and-tenon joinery and rigid back panels) are generally unnecessary.

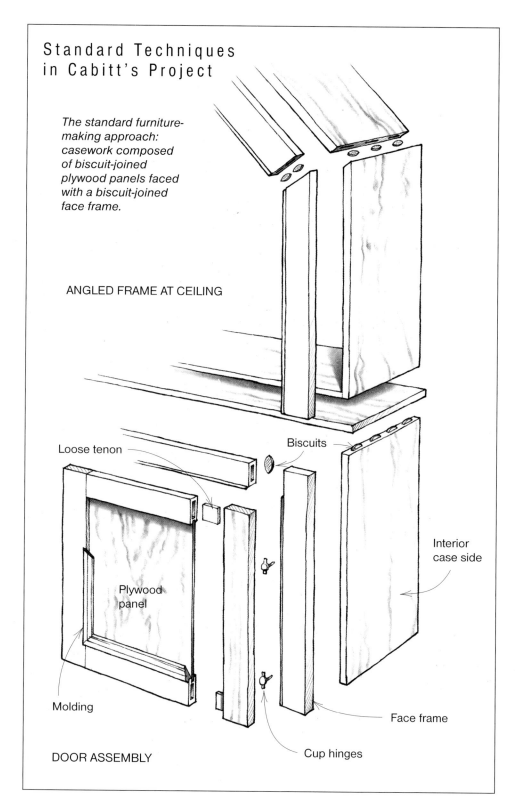

Standard Techniques in Cabitt's Project

The standard furniture-making approach: casework composed of biscuit-joined plywood panels faced with a biscuit-joined face frame.

ANGLED FRAME AT CEILING

Loose tenon

Biscuits

Plywood panel

Interior case side

Molding

Cup hinges

Face frame

DOOR ASSEMBLY

The all-mahogany library wall system shown in the photo on p. 32 was built with typical modern furniture-making techniques. Stephen Cabitt, of Rowley, Massachusetts, who designed and built this furnishing, used plate-biscuit joinery for carcase, face-frame, and mantel components; loose tenons for door frames; molded panels; and European-style cup hinges (see the drawing at left).

For a contrasting approach, consider the wall system shown in the photo on the facing page. This system, which contains a desk/computer center, entertainment center, shelving, and storage cabinets, was designed by cabinetmaker Roger Benson, of Upton, Massachusetts, and built by Benson entirely on site. In a clear departure from typical case-component construction, Benson created the skeleton of the unit with a 2x4 framework constructed to meet the angled ceiling and to surround the window (see the drawing on the facing page). He then sheathed it with ¼-in. hardwood plywood panels to form the ceilings and backs of the unit. He switched to ¾-in. ply for some structural areas and to drywall to cover the soffit and the sides facing the window alcove.

Nontraditional Techniques in Benson's Project

The nontraditional approach: structure of furnishing created by facing a 2x4 framework.

2x4 ripped at 20° angle

Plywood

Cleat

Plywood

Side of box

Dado

Facing

Frame of 2x4s

2x4 frame

Roger Benson's wall unit was built on site by applying facing components to a 2x4 framework, as shown in the drawing at left. The clean lines and white painted surfaces visually reduce the imposing size of the unit. Photo by Shawn Cassidy.

Determining Dimensions

Because they must fit a given space, built-ins require special techniques to determine their dimensions in the design stage and to install them during the course of their construction. To size a built-in without creating a mind-numbing drawing crammed with lines and dimensions, I use story sticks. Simple in concept and straightforward to use, story sticks can establish the dimensions and assembly positions of all the components of the unit from the actual site situation (see the drawing below). And they are virtually foolproof.

Though any long scraps of straight stock will do for story sticks, I like to make them by ripping 1½-in.-wide strips from ¼-in. white-faced Masonite. The resulting "sticks" are straight and strong; they mark clearly and easily with a sharp pencil, and the slick white face erases easily for corrections. If I need lengths longer than 8 ft., I glue and staple two or more strips together. I make up three story sticks for the layout: one for horizontal, one for vertical, and one for depth.

To see how story sticks work, let's assume you are measuring an alcove for a built-in cabinet. To find the inside span of the alcove, make up a pair of story sticks with angled ends—I call these "slip

sticks." Hold the sticks together and push their angled ends against the opposite walls. When they touch, lock the sticks together by clamping them with C-clamps (Step 1 in the drawing on the facing page). Then locate the wall studs and mark their centerlines on the sticks (see the sidebar on p. 38). When you are done, tilt up the sticks and lift them carefully out of the alcove.

Before you can transfer the alcove's inside dimension to the horizontal layout story stick, you need to determine if there is any offset from square between the front of the alcove and its back wall. To do so, first hold a framing square against the stick (which you have laid

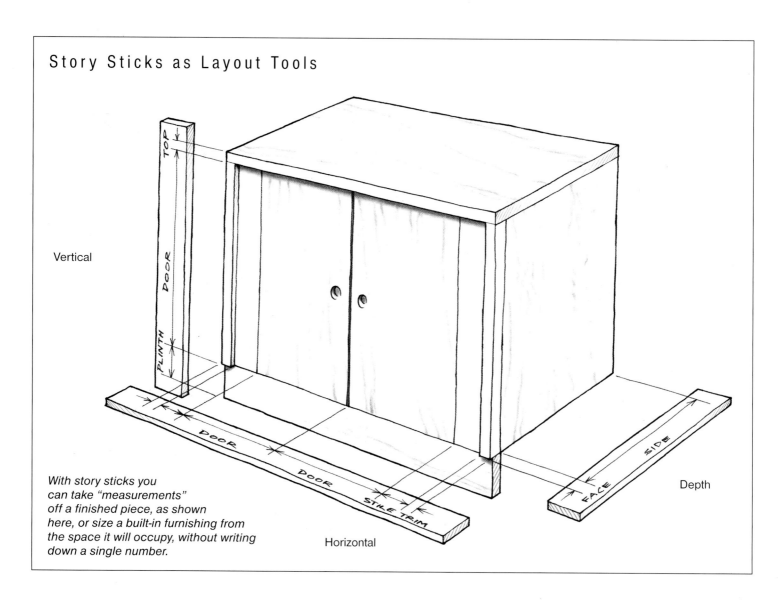

Story Sticks as Layout Tools

Vertical

TOP

DOOR

PLINTH

DOOR

DOOR

DOOR STILE TRIM

Horizontal

FACE

SIDE

Depth

With story sticks you can take "measurements" off a finished piece, as shown here, or size a built-in furnishing from the space it will occupy, without writing down a single number.

Transferring Site Dimensions to a Story Stick

1. MEASURE THE INTERIOR SPAN WITH SLIP STICKS

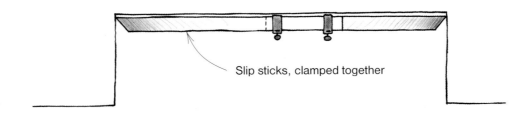

Slip sticks, clamped together

Place sticks in back of alcove, slide against side walls, and clamp sticks together with a C-clamp. Check at various heights to find the smallest span. Be sure to hold sticks level.

2. DETERMINE THE OFFSET BETWEEN THE OUTSIDE OPENING AND THE BACK WALL

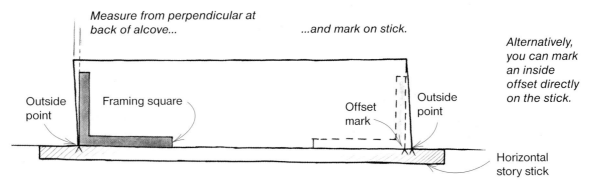

Measure from perpendicular at back of alcove...

...and mark on stick.

Alternatively, you can mark an inside offset directly on the stick.

Outside point

Framing square

Offset mark

Outside point

Horizontal story stick

Hold the horizontal story stick across the face of the opening and mark the outside points of the alcove. Then hold a framing square against the stick and note the offset from perpendicular.

3. TRANSFER THE INSIDE SPAN TO THE HORIZONTAL STORY STICK

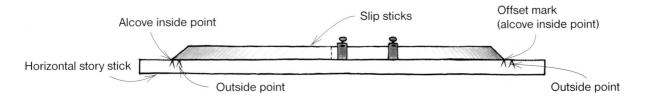

Alcove inside point

Slip sticks

Offset mark (alcove inside point)

Horizontal story stick

Outside point

Outside point

Align the right-hand point of the slip sticks with the offset mark (which is also the alcove inside point), and transfer the alcove inside-point mark from the left-hand point of the slip sticks to the horizontal story stick.

The easiest way to find a framing stud hidden behind drywall or other wall coverings is to slide an electronic sensing device across the surface. Most models announce the presence of a stud with lights; some make a noise as well. Follow the manufacturer's instructions to calibrate the unit for a particular type of covering, and keep the base of the detector flat against the wall as you move it slowly along the length of the wall or ceiling. Be aware that low battery power significantly reduces performance and can cause false readings.

Dramatically cheaper—though more time-consuming and unpredictable in use—is the old-fashioned magnetic nail finder. Nothing more than a magnet under glass, this tool indicates the presence of a stud by detecting the nails that secure the wall covering to the underlying framework. Find the nails by holding the base of the finder against the wall and then moving it in a circular motion. Spiral outward into larger circles until you notice the magnet swinging toward the wall—you've found your first nail. Search for other nails along a straight line running in the assumed direction of the framing. If you find a second nail, you have likely discovered a stud (or other framing member). Other studs will commonly be found at standard distances away (usually 16 in. or 24 in. on center).

While some experienced tradesmen swear you can find underlying framing by the sound it makes when you tap over it with your knuckles, there is one way to know for sure: Drive in a nail and see if it hits something solid (do this where the built-in will later cover the hole). If water doesn't come out of the nail hole, there is a good bet that you've hit a stud rather than some plumbing!

If the nail hits nothing, don't despair—try the electrician's trick shown in the drawing below, which works for uninsulated partition walls: Bend a piece of 24-in. length of stiff wire (coat-hanger wire is perfect) into a U shape. Insert one end into the hole left by the nail, then rotate the wire until it hits against a stud. The exposed leg of the U indicates exactly what is going on inside the wall, enabling you to mark the location of the stud on the outside of the wall.

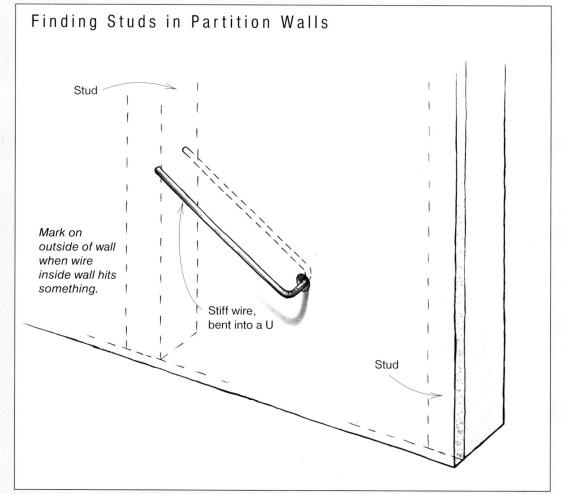

Finding Studs in Partition Walls

Stud

Mark on outside of wall when wire inside wall hits something.

Stiff wire, bent into a U

Stud

Layout of All Components on a Horizontal Story Stick

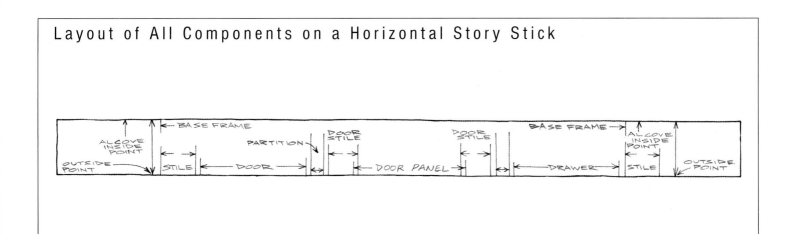

across the face of the alcove) and the left-hand side wall to check the wall angle (Step 2 in the drawing on p. 37). If there is any offset from square, measure the amount and mark it on the stick. Then lay the slip sticks on the horizontal story stick, align the right-hand point to the offset mark, and lay out the inside span of the alcove (Step 3). If the sides of the alcove are perfectly square, the inside span will equal the distance between the two outside corners. Also transfer the wall-stud centerline positions and the location of any utility outlets, heating ducts, and other objects or obstructions.

Having established the on-site dimensions, you can then lay out the position of all the components of the unit on the horizontal story stick (see the drawing above). Referring to your working drawing (which shows the overall configuration of the unit), mark out the precise length of the horizontal components and the position of all vertical components. In like manner, lay out the heights of the components on the vertical stick and the depths on the depth stick. You can continue to use the sticks to lay out the individual door components.

Once all the components are laid out on the three sticks, transfer their dimensions to a set of cut lists (samples are shown in the illustration above right).

Typical Cut Lists and Bills of Material

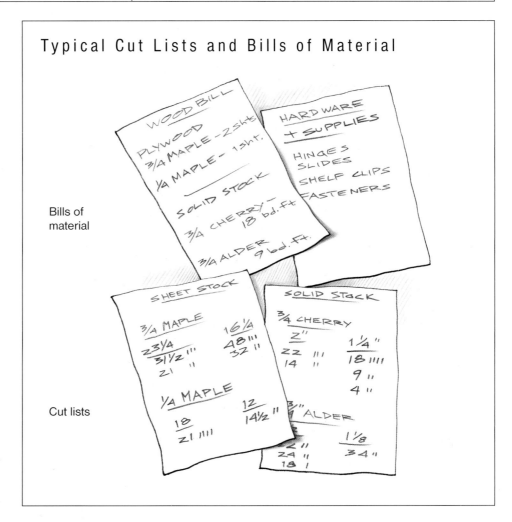

Bills of material

Cut lists

I usually make one list for sheet stock materials and another for solid stock. From these lists compile a bill of materials (adding hardware and other miscellaneous items) to take to the store.

Modifying a Load-bearing Wall for a Built-in

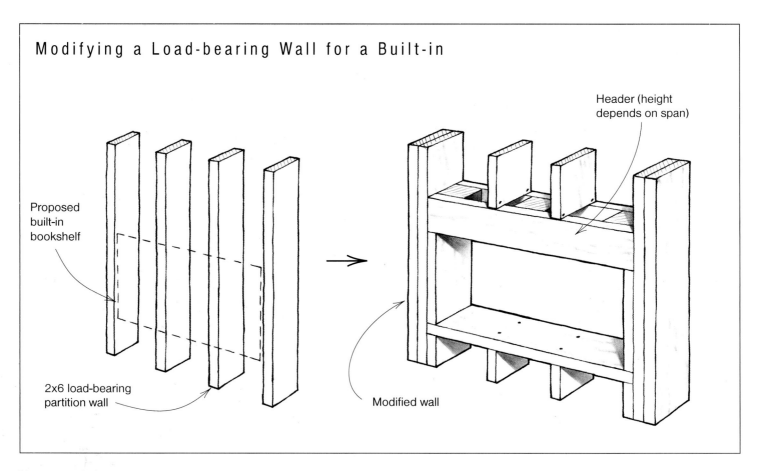

Proposed built-in bookshelf

2x6 load-bearing partition wall

Header (height depends on span)

Modified wall

You can mark the precise location of ledgers on a wall by transferring the layout lines from the vertical story stick. Photo by Craig Wester.

Installation Techniques

Generally, the first thing to do before installing a built-in is to prepare the structural wall surfaces. First, be sure that the wall covering (usually drywall) sits flat and is well secured to the under-lying studs. If the wall has been newly drywalled, you can use a Surform or sanding machine to smooth away any lumps in the mudding. Also check for solid backing in the areas of the wall to which ledgers will be attached. If the backing is inadequate, you can cover the entire wall behind the unit with $\frac{1}{2}$-in. plywood to provide ample nailing.

If the built-in is to be recessed into a load-bearing wall (usually an outside wall or a partition wall supporting floor joists), you may have to remove the wall cover-ing and install more framing material (see the drawing above). Unless you are well versed in house framing, I suggest that you consult first with an experienced carpenter or building engineer to plan any modifications to the framing.

To locate the placement of ledgers designed to support some of the case components, use the vertical story stick to mark the height location (see the photo on the facing page) and a carpenter's level to draw a level line. Because the floor may not be level, install the base frame first. Cut the story stick at the appropriate place so you can rest the bottom end on the leveled base. Install the ledgers by screwing them to the underlying studs. To locate vertical nailers on the back wall of the alcove, use the slip sticks (with marks transferred from the horizontal stick).

Sometimes a built-in has to fill the entire space between the floor and ceiling of a room—and as most cabinet-makers have long discovered, floors and ceilings are rarely parallel to one another. This was certainly true for Bill Walker, of Seattle, Washington, who built and installed the full-height furnishing shown in the photo below in a Seattle condominium. Not only was the floor

To fit this built-in kitchen peninsula/living-room cupboard and shelf system precisely between the floor and the ceiling, builder Bill Walker scribed the base frame to meet the floor line and then used slip sticks to determine the height (at a number of points) to the ceiling. Photo by Craig Wester.

A shelving unit by John and Carolyn Grew-Sheridan fills the alcove next to a living-room fireplace. Scribed to fit, the generously sized trim moldings join the unit to the existing walls of the room. Photo by John Grew-Sheridan.

not parallel with the soffit installed by the contractor, but the design, by Weinstein Copeland Architects, of Seattle, Washington, called for precise ½-in. inset shadow lines where the cabinets meet the baseboard and soffit as well as crisp ⅛-in. reveals between the doors and fixed panels.

To install this built-in so that the variance between the floor and ceiling would be undetectable, Walker followed these steps: First, he set the base frame on the floor, using shims to hold the frame perfectly level (Step 1 in the drawing at right). Then, using a compass, he scribed the out-of-level floor line to the side of the base frame (Step 2). Having cut the base frame to the line, he could then fasten it to the floor—the bottom edge meets the floor line while the top edge sits level (Step 3). Next, Walker used slip sticks (Step 4) at a series of points along the run of the frame to determine the vertical span between the top of the base frame and the underside of the soffit. Knowing these spans, he could then adjust the length of the vertical partitions of the display shelving so they would fill the span while leaving a uniform ½-in.-wide shadow line just below the soffit.

A more forgiving way in which a built-in can join with the architectural elements of a room is illustrated by the living-room shelving unit shown in the photo on the facing page and designed and built by John and Carolyn Grew-Sheridan, of San Francisco, California. Because the unit is surrounded with a wide band of flat-faced molding, it required only a relatively simple process of scribing to cut and join the moldings flush with the wall and ceiling. Variations in molding width that resulted from the scribe are undetectable, even to the most discerning eye.

Dimensioning Parts to Run between Floor and Ceiling

1. Shim the base frame level.

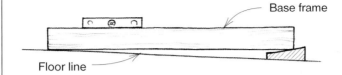

Base frame

Floor line

2. Scribe a line to transfer the floor profile to the base frame.

Compass

3. Cut the base frame to the line and install.

Top edge is level.

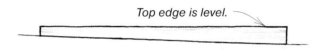

4. Take height readings with slip sticks at a series of points.

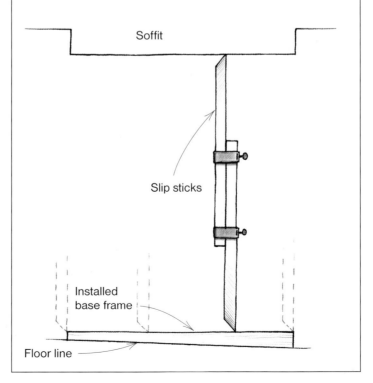

Soffit

Slip sticks

Installed base frame

Floor line

To scribe a stile to fit between a fixed point on a piece of casework and a wall surface, follow this sequence of steps, as shown in the drawing below:

Cut the stile to length and set it by the wall unit. Now, adjust the arms of a scribing compass at the distance (width) between a point on the installed casework representing the inside edge of the stile and the wall surface. Do this at two locations—one near the top and one near the bottom of the stile. Transfer these width settings to the face of the board. (Step 1)

Now hold the stile against the case, and readjust the span of the scribe arms to overhang the edge of the stile about 1 in. when held to the innermost mark. Adjust the position of the stile so that the scribe point just touches the wall when the other point touches the innermost mark. Do this at both the top and bottom marks (Step 2). Drive finish nails or use double-stick tape to hold the board temporarily in place at this location.

Draw the line representing the wall surface down the face of the stile (Step 3). You must hold the compass points level as you draw the line.

Cut the stile along the scribe line (Step 4). To create a gap-free juncture, make the cut with a back bevel of 2°

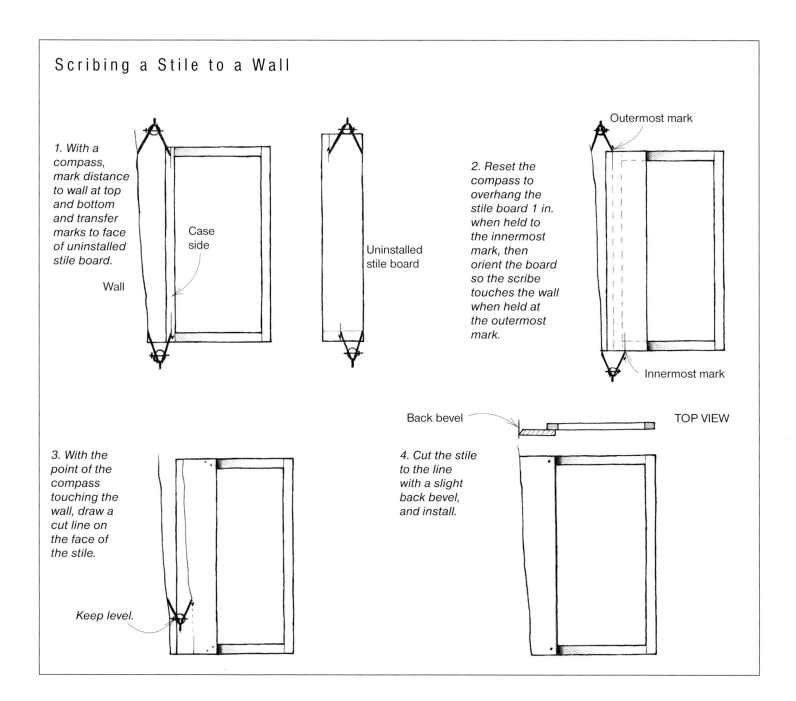

Scribing a Stile to a Wall

1. With a compass, mark distance to wall at top and bottom and transfer marks to face of uninstalled stile board.

Wall

Case side

Uninstalled stile board

2. Reset the compass to overhang the stile board 1 in. when held to the innermost mark, then orient the board so the scribe touches the wall when held at the outermost mark.

Outermost mark

Innermost mark

3. With the point of the compass touching the wall, draw a cut line on the face of the stile.

Keep level.

4. Cut the stile to the line with a slight back bevel, and install.

Back bevel

TOP VIEW

to 3°. When installing the stile, force the sharp edge into the meeting surface.

Scribing really comes in handy when you have to fit a built-in cabinet to a highly irregular surface. Cabinetmaker John Marckworth, of Port Townsend, Washington, made good use of scribing technique when he installed a cabinet against a stone chimney (see the photo at right).

What happens when you have to fit a component of a built-in to not one wall surface, but three? This was the situation confronted by Don Williams, of Williamson, New York, when installing the seat board of a long window seat shown in the photo below. The single Southern pine top board of the seat had to fit precisely against the three surrounding surfaces, so Williams made a cutting pattern. The sidebar on pp. 46-47 explains a couple of approaches the cabinetmaker can take.

Scribing allowed this cabinet to fit tightly against a stone chimney. Photo by John Marckworth.

The top board of this window seat had to fit against three surrounding surfaces, so the builder made a cutting pattern. Photo by Don Williams.

Here are two ways to achieve a perfect fit with your built-ins. Both involve making cutting patterns. I use the Joe Frogger Method for complex cuts or if curved cuts are involved. The Jigger Stick Method is a bit simpler and is effective when you only need to make a series of relatively long, straight cuts.

JOE FROGGER METHOD

The Joe Frogger Method, taught to me by the late boatbuilder Bud McIntosh (1990s sensibilities preclude my telling you where the name came from), requires nothing more than a scrap piece of cardboard, a square block of wood (the frog), and a pen or pencil. Done carefully, this method allows you to transfer the most complex shapes to the workpiece with speed and unfailing precision.

Begin by cutting a piece of cardboard about 1 in. shy of the perimeter to be filled by the workpiece (depending on the situation, you may need to support the cardboard on a temporary filler board such as a scrap of plywood cut to the rough shape.) Hold the cardboard in place with tape or thumbtacks (Step 1 in the photo series at right).

Next hold the frog against the wall and mark the opposite edge on the cardboard (Step 2), using a sharp pencil or fine pen. Continue to make a series of marks, spacing

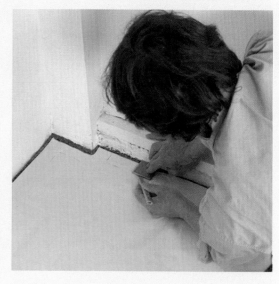

1. Tape a cardboard pattern on a temporary filler board for support.

2. Mark the outside edge of the frog on the cardboard at a series of points.

3. With the pattern taped to the workpiece, hold the frog to the marks on the pattern and mark the workpiece on the opposite side.

4. Connect the marks on the workpiece to form the cut line. Photos by Craig Wester.

them closely on curves, farther apart on straight runs. If you have to cut around a projection, be sure to mark each side.

When you finish marking, lift away the cardboard and tape it to the workpiece. Now reverse the process, holding the frog to the marks on the pattern and marking along the

opposite side of the frog, which sits on the workpiece (Step 3).

Finally connect the marks on the workpiece (Step 4). Use a straightedge on straight runs and a flexible batten—a ¼-in. square strip of oak is ideal—on curves. If you cut precisely to this line, you should get a near-perfect fit.

JIGGER STICK METHOD

The Jigger Stick Method, so named because of the "jiggers" cut along one side of the stick, works in essentially the same way as the Joe Frogger Method. However, because tracing the stick is rather time-consuming—and could lead to a confusion of lines on the template—the Jigger Stick Method is more useful for situations with no curves or complex projections.

Begin by laying the cardboard pattern in place on site (Step 1 in the photo series at right).

Set the jigger stick with its pointed end touching a point—usually a corner. Using a sharp pencil, trace the outline of the stick where it lies over the cardboard (Step 2). Repeat the process at each corner of the site.

When all the points are marked, pick up the cardboard and tape it to the workpiece. Now set the stick within its outlines and mark the points on the workpiece (Step 3).

Continue until you have created a "connect-the-dot" image of the site. This is your cut line (Step 4).

1. The cardboard pattern and jigger stick.

2. Trace the outline of the jigger stick at various points.

3. Tape the pattern to the workpiece, place the stick within the outlines, and mark the points on the workpiece.

4. Connect the marks on the workpiece to form the cut line. Photos by Craig Wester.

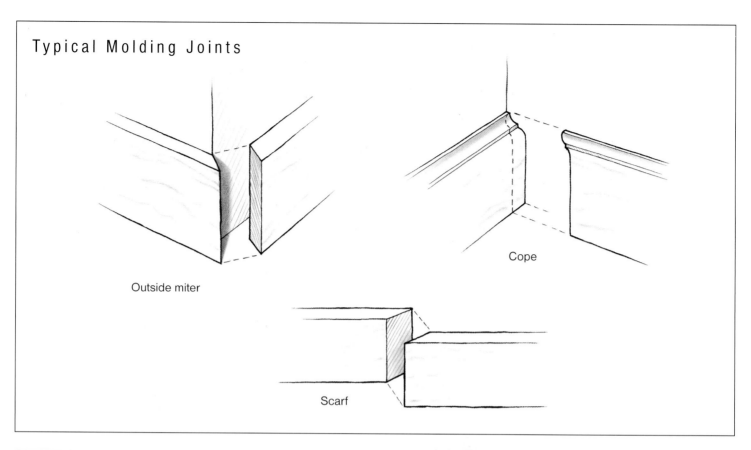

Typical Molding Joints

Outside miter

Cope

Scarf

Cope, miter, and scarf joints fit the cornice molding to Bill Irvine's wall-to-wall and floor-to-floor library shelving unit. Photo by Craig Wester.

Once the basic structure of a built-in piece of casework is in place, the last steps in the installation often involve installing moldings that tie the furnishing to those already in the room. The three essential joints for accomplishing this—the outside miter, the cope, and the scarf—are shown in the drawing above. Use the miter when joining moldings at an outside corner. At inside corners, use the cope joint. (Unlike the alternative inside miter joint, the cope joint stays tight and hides any evidence of movement between the two moldings.) If you have to extend the molding—for example, when running the cornice across the front of the top frieze board of the built-in—join the new molding to the old with a scarf joint. In the built-in shown in the photo at left, cabinetmaker Bill Irvine, of Port Townsend, Washington, has made ample use of all these joints to install the cornice molding that ties the shelving units to the room's ceilings.

TOOLS FOR CONSTRUCTING AND INSTALLING BUILT-IN FURNISHINGS

STATIONARY POWER TOOLS

- Table saw with accurate rip fence and commercial or shop-made sliding crosscut table
- Jointer
- Lightweight 10-in. or 12-in. surface planer
- Drill press
- Dust collector (optional)
- Radial-arm saw or sliding compound-miter saw
- Bandsaw
- Air compressor (for applying finish and driving pneumatic fasteners)

PORTABLE POWER TOOLS

- Drill (at least one ¼-in. or ⅜-in. variable-speed, reversing drill—9.6 volt, or greater; cordless are fine for cabinetmaking)
- Power screwdriver (9.6-volt cordless impact driver recommended)
- Sanders (one belt and at least one square-base orbital) or random-orbit sander
- Routers (3-hp table-mounted router, 1-hp plunge router, and laminate trimmer)
- Circular saw (with optional cutting guides)
- Jigsaw
- Reciprocal saw
- Biscuit joiner
- Pneumatic tacker/nailer
- Air-sprayer finish applicator (optional)
- Hand-operated heat-gun edgebander (optional)

HAND TOOLS

Layout tools

- 16-ft. tape measure
- 24-in. framing square
- 12-in. combination square
- Water level, builder's level, or laser level
- 48-in., 24-in., and torpedo bubble levels
- Architect's rule
- Bevel gauge
- Contour gauge
- Plumb bob
- Compass scribe, trammel points
- Marking knife, awl, chalk, pencils, and sharpener
- Layout template/drill guide for shelf holes (optional)

Cutting tools

- Set of handsaws for ripping and crosscutting (Japanese combination saw recommended)
- Miter box (for joining moldings)
- Compass saw and hacksaw
- Hole saws
- Set of chisels
- Block, rabbet, and jack planes
- Drill bits, countersink, and plug-cutting bits; router bits

Fastening tools

- Set of screwdrivers
- Hammers (13-in. claw, tack, and rubber mallet)
- Nail set
- Nail remover
- Jig for hand-drilling pocket holes (optional)
- Jig for drilling dowel holes (optional)

Holding and grasping tools

- Wood vise
- Pipe clamps (at least one pair each with 24-in., 36-in., and 48-in. capacities)
- Parallel-jaw bar clamps, dimensions as above (optional)
- Pair of 5-in. C-clamps
- Pliers, wrench
- Socket set
- Vise-grip clamp (optional) to align frame stock for pocket-hole assembly

Finishing tools

- Cabinet scraper
- Hand files
- Glue scraper
- Drop cloth
- Surform
- Caulk gun
- Putty knives (for applying fillers)
- Shaped sanding blocks and assortment of sandpaper

Miscellaneous

- Portable workbench and vise
- Glue applicator (with optional nozzle for biscuit slots)
- Roller for pressing down laminate
- Electronic stud finder
- Scissors jack (for installing wall cabinets)
- Stand-mounted lights
- Extension cords
- Stepladder
- First-aid kit

Built-in furnishings create a rich, warm welcome in this circular foyer, which was designed by Louis Mackall (view is toward the entry door). For more on this project, see p. 52. Photo by Louis Mackall.

4

FOYERS AND
LIVING ROOMS

Now that we've seen how built-ins are designed, constructed, and installed, it's time to start our room-by-room tour of the house. Beginning with the foyer and then moving into the living room, we'll see how built-in furnishings—whether filling entire walls, creating boundaries between rooms, or simply offering display spaces—define both the aesthetics and the function of these rooms.

Display shelving built into a passageway off the foyer draws you toward the living room. Photo by Louis Mackall.

Three Entryways

Welcome home! An elegant foyer encircled with built-in furnishings (see the photos at left and on p. 50) is the first thing you encounter when you enter this New York City apartment. Unlike stand-alone furniture, the benches, cupboards, and display shelves that surround you are integral to the roomscape. These furnishings inform you that this is a room with a life and function of its own, not just a place on the way to somewhere else. The passage from the foyer into the living room is particularly delightful: The flanking built-in cases encourage you to linger to enjoy the artwork displayed within their softly lighted interiors.

It was the job of architect Louis Mackall, of Guilford, Connecticut, to convert this once dark and forbidding cubicle buried in the center of the apartment to such a welcoming space. Redesigned into a circular shape, the foyer can now welcome light from the rest of the apartment—the curved walls help to reflect the light evenly around the room. As can be seen in the before/after floor plans on the facing page, Mackall carefully oriented the doors to create new sight lines, drawing the eye from the center of the foyer to the outermost periphery of the apartment. Compare the new arrangement to the original floor plan, which had all the charm of a dungeon. The project was built by Breakfast Woodworks, also of Guilford.

Mackall's Circular Foyer

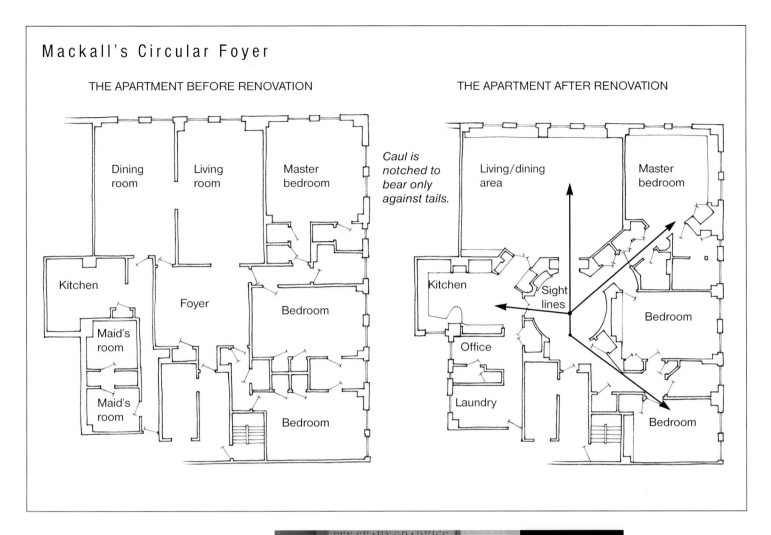

THE APARTMENT BEFORE RENOVATION

Dining room

Living room

Master bedroom

Kitchen

Foyer

Bedroom

Maid's room

Maid's room

Bedroom

Caul is notched to bear only against tails.

THE APARTMENT AFTER RENOVATION

Living/dining area

Master bedroom

Kitchen

Sight lines

Bedroom

Office

Laundry

Bedroom

Sometimes just a small touch is enough to lend elegance to an entry. In Seattle architect Ed Weinstein's own home, a subtle built-in glass shelf greets visitors with a miniature gallery of art. The glass fills the recess created to the side of the stairs (see the photo at right), underlining the hanging artwork and providing a shelf for flower arrangements. To support the shelf as well as the handrail, builder Bill Walker, of Seattle, Washington, ran bolts through the handrail, through the hollow stainless-steel tubes that cradle the shelf, and into the wall studs.

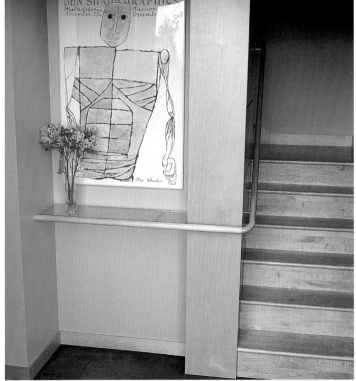

A glass shelf tucked behind the handrail adds visual interest to Ed Weinstein's otherwise spartan staircase entryway. Photo by Craig Wester.

Built-in shelving with reed baskets as organizers fills one wall of Tom Bosworth's entry hall. Photo by Craig Wester.

Architect Tom Bosworth, of Seattle, Washington, designed the entryway to his home with practicality and economy of space foremost in mind. He created a recessed area right next to the door and filled it floor to ceiling with shelving (see the photo at left). Baskets organize and help ease access to the gardening implements, hats, gloves, and sporting equipment that are stored there. A small wine rack also finds a home in this relatively cool space. The shelving was built by Ravenhill Construction, of Friday Harbor, Washington.

Great Rooms

Reminiscent of the great rooms of ancient castles, huge living rooms are popular in even the most contemporary residential buildings. The challenge for designers is to create an expansive, elegant room that can still offer its inhabitants a feeling of warmth, cheer, and coziness. One good solution, as exemplified in a 22-ft. by 46-ft. living room created by architect Louis Mackall, of Guilford, Connecticut, relies heavily on extensive built-in furnishings.

In the room, shown in the photo on the facing page, the length of an entire wall is composed of built-in cabinetry: cupboards below, with display shelving behind glass doors above. The opposite wall is filled with windows, French doors, and a magnificent fireplace and mantel. Comfortable couches and a huge coffee table fill the space between. The soft interior lighting of the display cases, the low-voltage lighting strung across the room, and the glow of the fireplace bathe the room in a cozy amber radiance. With the display units filled with art, the wall takes on the appearance of a three-dimensional mural—a wall full of rich visual excitement.

One entire wall of this expansive living room, designed by Louis Mackall, is framed deep
enough to house a floor-to-ceiling run of built-in cabinetry made of painted MDF and poplar.
The counters and mantel are mahogany. Photo by Louis Mackall.

Maple-veneered built-ins define the opposing walls of a great room in a Seattle lakefront home designed by Weinstein Copeland Architects. (See the facing page for the mantel detail.) Photos by Craig Wester.

A great room designed by Weinstein Copeland Architects with Bill Walker, all of Seattle, Washington, though on the opposite coast of the United States, has a similar layout—and much the same ambience—as Mackall's great room. The sitting area (see the photos on the facing page) is flanked by built-ins: on one side, a fireplace surround featuring built-in cabinetry running below a full-length, gently curving mantel, and on the other side, a floor-to-ceiling wall unit housing glass display shelving.

Bill Walker, who was also the builder, constructed the 13-ft.-long mantel by applying maple veneer and solid-wood edging to a core built up of plywood sandwiched around a solid-wood framework. As shown in the drawing below, bolts passing through the back rail of the interior framework secure the mantel to the wall framing. After applying the solid-wood facing to the edge and ends of the core assembly, Walker formed its curved and angled profile with power and hand planes, followed by a cabinet scraper.

The unit creates a wall between the living room and kitchen—on the kitchen side the unit provides upper and lower cupboard space. The back of the display-shelf unit protrudes into the kitchen,

Mantel Detail

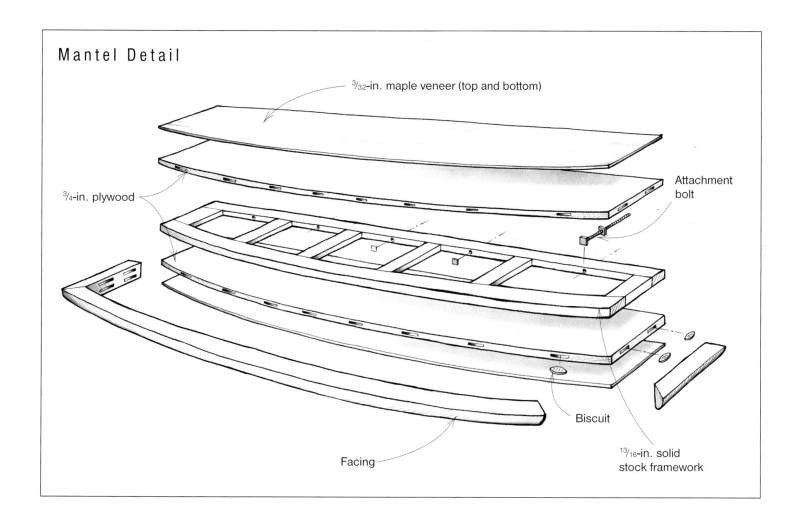

$^3/_{32}$-in. maple veneer (top and bottom)

$^3/_4$-in. plywood

Attachment bolt

Biscuit

Facing

$^{13}/_{16}$-in. solid stock framework

providing a surface for a well-used bulletin board (see the photo and drawing below).

To create the large maple surfaces of both the mantel-side cabinetry and the wall unit/display case Walker applied maple veneer over a panel-stock substrate. (One way to apply veneers is described in the sidebar on pp. 60-61.) To create the fine shadow lines around the panels, he ran a flush-trim bit fit with an undersized guide bearing along the edge of the panel to produce a precise, tiny rabbet. A groove—or shadow line—is formed when this rabbeted panel butts against a straight-edged panel.

In the great room of a residence with a vaulted ceiling, architect Peter Bethanis, of Kents Hill, Maine, decided to take maximum advantage of the space created by the overhang of the stairway landing. Using the same wood (pickled oak) for the cabinetry as for the stairway components and entry door, Bethanis filled the space with a mix of open shelving, storage cupboards, drawers, and two desks (see the photo on the facing page). To reduce visual clutter, he had cabinetmaker David Lancaster, of Weeksmill, Maine, install bifold doors to conceal the desk surfaces. Stereo equipment is behind the large double-doors of the center cabinet.

This is the kitchen-side view of the wall shown in the bottom photo on p. 56 (a cross-sectional drawing is shown at right). Photo by Craig Wester.

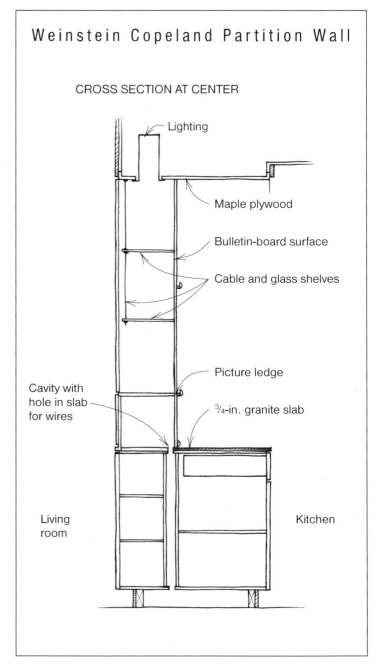

Weinstein Copeland Partition Wall

CROSS SECTION AT CENTER

Lighting

Maple plywood

Bulletin-board surface

Cable and glass shelves

Picture ledge

Cavity with hole in slab for wires

$^3/_4$-in. granite slab

Living room

Kitchen

Filling almost the entire wall of a great room, Peter Bethanis's full-story-height cabinetwork
appears to support an overhanging stair landing. Photo © Brian Vanden Brink.

Though maple-faced plywoods are available "off the shelf," the only way you can ensure good grain matching across a broad surface is to select and apply the veneer yourself. Also, because hand-applied veneer is substantially thicker than most plywood face veneers, the figure (especially the quilted patterns in some maples) looks dramatically deeper and richer. For discriminating woodworkers and their clients, the difference is well worth the additional effort.

Here is one good way to veneer your own panels:

After cutting the panels to size, the first task in the veneering process is to clamp and glue a solid-wood edging to the exposed edges of the substrate (Step 1 in the drawing below). An industrial-grade (HD, or high-density) particleboard makes a good substrate for cabinet doors, and MDF, which is less predictably flat, can be used for supported surfaces. If the panel is structural (i.e., it supports a load), use a void-free hardwood plywood. When the glue is dry, you can use a shop-made fixture to guide the panel past a flush-trim bit installed on a table-mounted router (Step 2).

Next is bookmatching (Step 3) and aligning the veneers on the panel to create an appealing and uniform grain match—both on the panel itself and in relation to the surrounding panels. To ensure a good joint, make the cut along a straightedge, cutting through both veneers at once. If any voids show

Veneering a Panel

Step 1: Apply edging to substrate.

Step 3: "Open" veneers, which were cut and stacked in sequence, to create bookmatch.

Step 2: Trim edging flush to substrate on a table-mounted router.

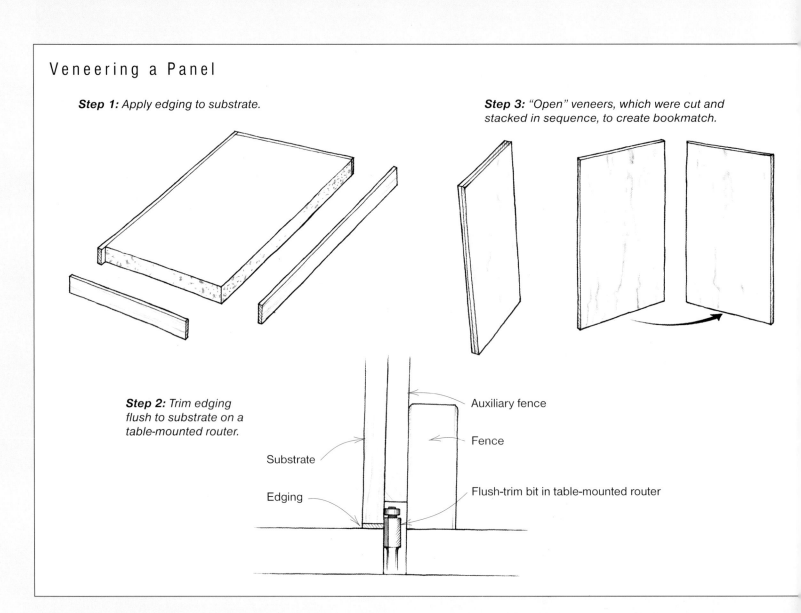

Substrate

Edging

Auxiliary fence

Fence

Flush-trim bit in table-mounted router

when you hold the veneers together edge to edge, plane both edges at the same time on a shooting board (Step 4). Then tape the veneers together with special veneer tape .

The next step (Step 5) assumes the use of glue film to apply the veneer—the simplest system for a small shop. If you are set up for it, however, you can apply liquid glue and clamp the veneer to the substrate with a veneer press or vacuum-bag system.

Cut the glue film slightly larger than the panel and attach it to the substrate with an iron set on medium heat. When the glue has set, peel off the backing sheet. Now align the bookmatched veneers on the substrate, cover them with the backing sheet and press the veneer into the glue film with the iron (Step 6). Press down firmly behind the iron with a block of wood or veneer hammer. Work out from the middle toward the edges. If you get a bubble, make a small incision along the grain with a razor to let the air escape. Finally, trim off the overhanging veneer with a small router or laminate trimmer fitted with a flush-trim bit.

Caution: if the panel is free-floating, such as a cabinet door, be sure to apply veneer to both sides of the substrate to minimize warp. To save on costs, you can get away with applying a less expensive veneer such as alder or poplar, to the inside.

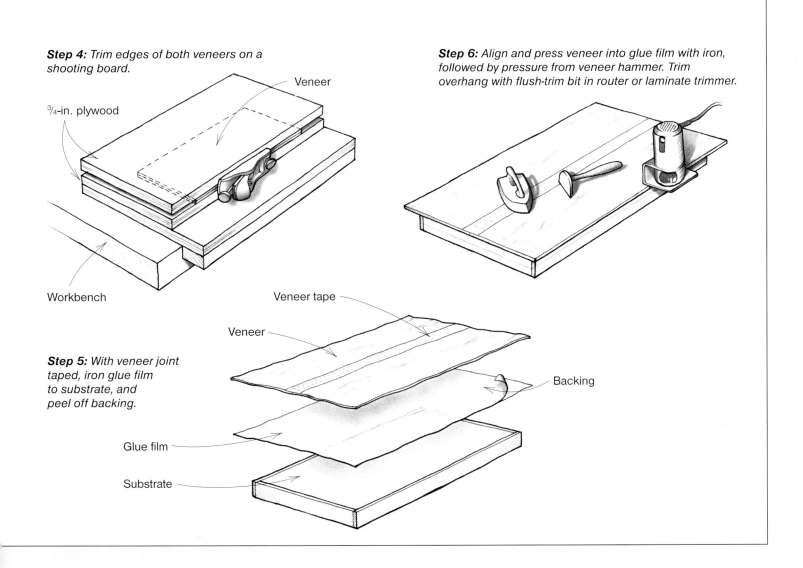

Step 4: *Trim edges of both veneers on a shooting board.*

Veneer

³/₄-in. plywood

Workbench

Step 6: *Align and press veneer into glue film with iron, followed by pressure from veneer hammer. Trim overhang with flush-trim bit in router or laminate trimmer.*

Veneer tape

Veneer

Backing

Step 5: *With veneer joint taped, iron glue film to substrate, and peel off backing.*

Glue film

Substrate

Art display shelving by Lawrence Cheng eloquently fills the space between a post and a curved wall. Photo © Brian Vanden Brink.

Built-ins for Display

As you have already seen, designers often take advantage of built-in shelving and cabinetry to create display spaces for artwork and other collectibles. In the examples shown here, the furnishing exits solely for the sake and safety of the art. A built-in will protect the artwork if it is accidentally bumped into by someone—an occurrence far more probable with stand-alone tables and shelves than with a built-in furnishing.

Consider the built-in shown in the top photo at left. The designer, architect Lawrence Cheng, of Cambridge, Massachusetts, filled the short partition wall jutting out from the end of a curved wall surface with floor-to-ceiling glass shelves. The choice of glass is clearly appropriate for art display—seen only as a subtle translucent-green line on edge, it does not distract from the objects it supports. Clear glass also allows the downlighting in the alcove's ceiling to travel through to the lowest shelves. The shelving was built by Cold Mountain Builders of Belfast, Maine.

D. Ralph Katz, of Cranbury, New Jersey, filled an entire wall of a living room with a furnishing that would dramatically showcase the owner's artwork—and make an architectural statement on its own (see the bottom photo at left). Impressive columns (made from humble PVC sewer pipe spray-painted with black lacquer) frame a painting on one side and glass display shelving (with a mirror back) on the other. A credenza rides between the columns. The mantel was created by bolting a sheet of plate glass to the base of the hanging columns flanking the fireplace. The unit was built by Timberline Cabinets, also of Cranbury.

This wall unit, designed by D. Ralph Katz, is built of lacquered PVC pipe columns and Vitricor panels, creating a unique showcase for art. Photo by D. Ralph Katz.

Built-ins as Boundaries

Built-in furnishings lend a room much of its function and character—in fact, they create a space in which one can enjoy life: thus a living room. But built-ins can be more than simply fixtures set within the room itself. Cabinets placed at the room entrance help to define the space in relation to the surrounding rooms. They let you know you are entering a special place, a place of comfort and coziness separate from the tumult and traffic in the rest of the home.

Sylvestre Construction, of Minneapolis, Minnesota, reached back to the Craftsman era to find inspiration for a colonnade-style entrance to the remodeled living room of a 1924 farmhouse (see the top photo at right). Columns, supported on cupboards, flank the entrance, while a built-in credenza forms part of the wall that separates the living room from the dining room. Though the cabinet doors are hung with modern European-style cup hinges, a casual observer would never notice—they are painted black and do not show through the glass door panes. The result is a simple, yet elegant, welcome to a hearth-warmed living space.

In a more contemporary setting, designers Bruce Kranzburg and J. Matthew McMullen, of Boulder, Colorado, defined the separation between two living spaces with a pair of tall cabinets (see the bottom photo at right). Their height helps create a visual barrier and forms a corridor-like effect for the four-step stairway bridging the change in floor level. Notice how the built-in seating follows the curve of the stone wall—as do the drawer faces. The cabinets were built by BKI, Inc., also of Boulder.

Built-in cabinets and columns by Sylvestre Construction create a handsome boundary to a Craftsman-style living room. Photo by Frank Hesseffinger.

Tall flanking built-in cabinets, designed by Bruce Kranzburg and J. Matthew McMullen, clearly define the entrance to a raised library. Photo by Foto Imagery/Tim Murphy.

Samuel Van Dam's built-in cabinets and shelving form a wall between a kitchen and a living room. Photo © Brian Vanden Brink.

In a room designed by architect Samuel Van Dam, of Portland, Maine, and built by William Hall and Sons of Yarmouth, Maine, a wall-size piece of cabinetwork defines the boundary between two rooms: the living room and the kitchen. On the living-room side (see the photo above), the massive built-in furnishing offers bookshelves, cupboards and display shelving; on the kitchen side, there are cupboards. Because the unit does not extend to the ceiling, and since it incorporates a large pass-through, it does not sever the life of the kitchen from that of the living room. The

proportions of the pass-through are well thought out: it is large enough to allow casual exchange between the room residents, yet not so large that the living room is robbed of its coziness.

A pass-through is a good way to create a wall without a strict sense of barrier. While an aquarium is not exactly a pass-through, the effect is similar: One can see through the tank, and light can pass through and over the case. The room-dividing aquarium shown in the top photo on the facing page is filled with 250 gallons of saltwater and some sea critters. Full of life, this furnishing,

designed by Louise Haberfeld and Adiyan Haran of Evergreen, Colo., built by Haran and engineered by Ronald Barta, brings a feast to the senses when viewed from either side.

Room-dividing built-ins need not be floor to ceiling. The combination built-in bookshelf and seating system shown in the bottom photo on the facing page sweeps in a great curve across one end of a living room in a home designed by architect Louis Mackall of Guilford, Connecticut. Without creating a visual barrier, the unit (which was built by Breakfast Woodworks, also of Guilford)

A huge aquarium establishes a "living" wall between the entry and living areas of a home. Photo by Michael Fulks.

Right: A gracefully curved bookshelf/seating system by Louis Mackall separates a warm and cozy sunken living room from the entry hall. Photo by Robert Perron.

gently but firmly separates the cold functionality of the raised entry hall from the cozy intimacy of the sunken living area.

The semicircular shape of the built-in seating is well chosen: People can face each other comfortably, while the raised back creates a feeling of intimacy. Lights built into the unit provide warm downlighting on the seats and also shine upward through the glass set along the curved counter surface. The glass inserts help to lighten the visual effect of the oak wood counter, reducing its tendency (at this size and scale) to become an overpowering, massive presence.

The curved wall of this dining room is filled with cupboards and display alcoves. The shape of the alcoves hints at the architecture of ancient India—an effective complement to the artwork. Designed by Jefferson Riley of Centerbrook Architects and Planners of Essex, Conn., and built by Yoder and Sons of Middlefield, Ohio. Photo by Peter Mauss/Esto Photographics.

5

DINING ROOMS

Like the living room, the dining room provides ample opportunity for built-in furnishings—perhaps even more than the former because dining is generally relegated to one of the smaller rooms in a home. Built-ins thrive in small areas, for one of their primary benefits is saving space. Indeed, the cupboards of residential dining rooms have enjoyed a long tradition of being built as architectural furniture: Craftsman-era credenzas containing silverware and table linens were often recessed, fully or at least partially, into the dining-room wall (see pp. 6-7). Much earlier, triangular china hutches nestled into the corners of parlors, adding tremendous visual pleasure to the room for a minimum of space (see pp. 4-5). In contemporary home designs, practical and intimate daytime eating places such as breakfast nooks and lunch bars are often created entirely with built-ins.

From Coffers to Credenzas

In the European Middle Ages, the very idea of furniture began with chests—sturdy, box-shaped coffers designed to contain the private possessions of those lucky enough to possess any. In later centuries, these coffers would become cupboards, sprouting legs to raise them to a more convenient height. Those made specifically for communal eating rooms grew still higher and wider and were topped with a long, wide plank, evolving into what we now call a sideboard; the interiors contained the silverware and table linens, while the expansive top surface could augment the dining table, holding the bowls and platters of the great feasts. While the stand-alone sideboard still exists today, the built-in sideboard—commonly called a credenza ("a sideboard without legs," according to the Random House unabridged dictionary) is increasingly becoming a part of the visual language of contemporary architects and designer/builders.

Though a far cry in style from Jefferson Riley's built-in credenza design shown in the photo on p. 66, the rustic credenza shown below accomplishes a similar essential function: the economic, though visually pleasing, use of space. Extending along one wall of a porch-room dining area under a row of windows, this run of redwood cabinetry, which was designed by architect Peter Bohlin, of Pittsburgh, Pennsylvania, and built by Andreassen and Nicholson Construction, makes efficient use of an otherwise little-used space and holds tablecloths, napkins, silverware, and china. At the same time, its granite surface serves as a buffet table, allowing the dining table to be somewhat smaller (which opens up more space in the room). Using twig sections for door pulls was more than a flight of whimsy for Bohlin —the handles are a highly visible contribution to the rustic ambience of this Adirondack Mountain retreat.

When Elaine Ferguson, of Ojai, California, decided to turn the solarium of her own home into a dining room, she designed a credenza that wraps around the entire perimeter of the semicircular

Built-in credenza cabinetry by Peter Bohlin runs along one wall of the porch dining area in a rustic Adirondack home. A granite counter/buffet contributes to the ambience of a home filled with natural materials and motifs. Photo © Brian Vanden Brink.

space—making excellent use of the commonly misused or under-used area that exists under a run of windows (see the drawing at right and photo below). Filled with cupboards and some open shelving, this furnishing, which was built by Bill Batelaan, also of Ojai, makes a large volume of space available for storage, yet its narrow footprint keeps it from encroaching upon the room. The striking blue tile of the counter gives the room a cheery look and protects the wood from hot serving plates and from the inevitable drips of water weeping out of the hanging plants.

In the one area of the room faced with bricks instead of glass, a wall cabinet with leaded-glass doors creates a hutch-like effect. Drawers set below the

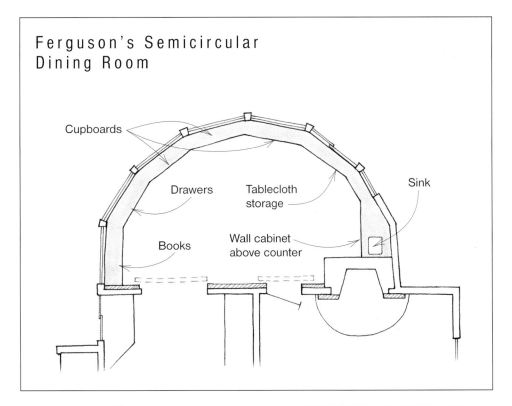

Ferguson's Semicircular Dining Room

Cupboards

Drawers

Tablecloth storage

Sink

Books

Wall cabinet above counter

Elaine Ferguson's credenza follows the perimeter of a semicircular dining room, making excellent use of the space under a run of windows, which is often wasted. Photo by Carol Topalian.

Rods set crosswise behind a pullout section of Ferguson's credenza hold tablecloths wrinkle free and instantly accessible. Photo by Carol Topalian.

counter in this area hold silverware. The small sink is conveniently located for rinsing dust off the dishes and for watering the plants.

One facet of the credenza features a fake double door. When you pull on the door you discover the face of a large slide-out bin (see the photo at left). Because Ferguson hates to iron, she designed this unique storage system—a row of closet poles—to hold tablecloths in a way that minimizes creasing. Another advantage of the pole system is that it instantly shows you the selection of cloths and makes them readily available—no need for removing or refolding linens to get at the tablecloth you want.

Cabinetmaker John Marckworth, of Port Townsend, Washington, designed and built the oak credenza shown in the photo below. Not only is the credenza attractive and practical, but it also forms

John Marckworth's long credenza forms a half-wall that separates the dining area from traffic through the entry hall. Photo by Craig Wester.

Andy Neumann's credenza of Honduras mahogany is recessed into the dining-room wall under a large pass-through into the kitchen. The drawers of the credenza contain silverware; table linens are stored behind the doors. Photo by Bill Zeldis.

a boundary between the dining room and the hall corridor that leads to the stairs and entry. Though the credenza is only a low peninsula, it creates a feeling of coziness in the eating area by maintaining a subtle but distinct sense of separation from the heavily traveled hallway. The furnishing features a wide, polished solid-wood top—an elegant surface on which to display plants and art objects. By carefully selecting the objects placed here, the degree of perceived separation can be controlled.

Architect Andy Neumann, of Carpinteria, California, designed a credenza that appears to be suspended under the black granite slab that flows out the pass-through from the kitchen (see the photo above). To allow for a more dramatic, larger-radius curve (and

to draw your eye to the flanking wall hangings), Neumann extended the counter surface well past the opening on both sides of the pass-through. He also asked the builder, Greg Erickson, of Santa Ynez, California, to bow the face of the credenza to a radius that matches the granite slab. Expanding further on the theme, Neumann reflected the credenza's curve in the hanging fixture over the dining table and in the backs of the chairs. Two large mahogany pocket doors with translucent glass can be pulled out of either side wall to separate the kitchen from the dining room, though they are usually left open so the cook can glimpse the ocean view out the dining-room window.

Designer Janice Smith, of Lawrence, Kansas, set a large structure of masonry

Janice Smith's massive masonry and wood furnishing featuring a multitude of shelves, counter surfaces, and a see-through fireplace separates the kitchen from the dining areas in a house with an open floor plan. The curved concrete hearth reflects the curved wall on the opposite side of the room. Photo by Janice Smith.

Floor Plan of Smith's House

and cabinetwork between the kitchen and dining areas of a house with an open floor plan, providing distinct boundaries and functions to both spaces (see the photo above). On the kitchen side, open storage shelving flanks the see-through fireplace; on the dining-area side, a credenza runs under a set of display shelves. The curved face of the credenza and the polished cement hearth relate to the curved wall of the dining area, helping tie the structure to the architecture of the home. The lighting, hidden behind the valance across the top of the shelving, bathes both rooms with diffuse light, making the structure itself appear less massive.

Smith's Room Divider

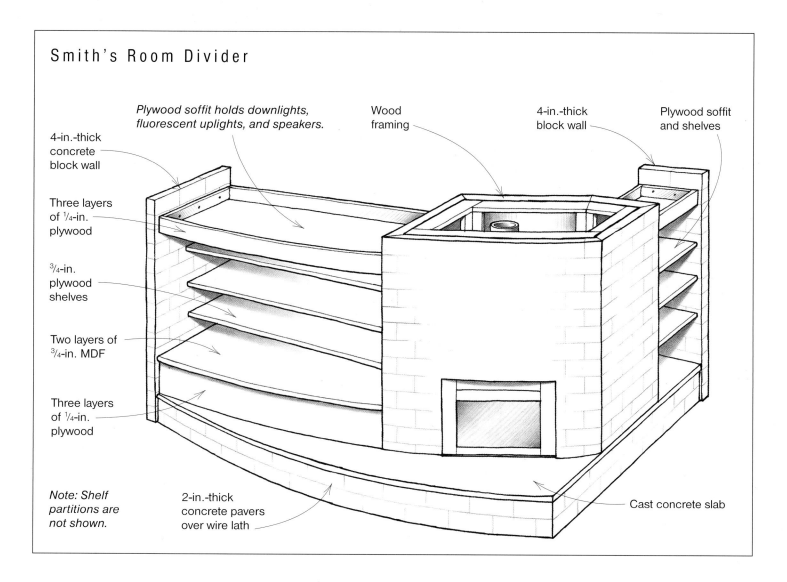

4-in.-thick concrete block wall

Three layers of ¼-in. plywood

¾-in. plywood shelves

Two layers of ¾-in. MDF

Three layers of ¼-in. plywood

Plywood soffit holds downlights, fluorescent uplights, and speakers.

Wood framing

4-in.-thick block wall

Plywood soffit and shelves

Note: Shelf partitions are not shown.

2-in.-thick concrete pavers over wire lath

Cast concrete slab

To reduce weight and ease construction, Smith opted not to have the masonry portion of the unit built of standard-sized concrete block. Instead, she designed an underlying framework of 2x4s to be sheathed with plywood (½-in. plywood on straight runs, ¼-in. plywood on curved areas). This framework was then veneered with 2-in.-thick concrete pavers. While the pavers have the same face dimensions as concrete block, they are much thinner (standard block is 12 in. thick). This makes them more appropriate for facing a curved surface such as the one below the hearth—the mortar between the vertical edges comes out much narrower. Pavers 4 in. thick form the end walls, and a sheet of ¾-in. plywood supports the poured slab that forms the hearth.

The woodwork is ¾-in. plywood edged with veneer tape and painted, except for the buffet top (which is two layered sheets of ¾-in. MDF) and the buffet's face (which is three glued layers of ¼-in. plywood). To secure the soffit assembly to the masonry, Smith drilled into the block and set anchors to receive the attachment bolts. Because she wanted invisible supports for the shelves, she cut the heads off the bolts and routed a groove in the underside of the shelf to slip over the bolt's protruding shank. The grooves were then puttied and painted.

China Cupboards

Paul Nuckols's reproduction of a traditional cockleshell corner cupboard recaptures the feel of an early, but elegant, Colonial parlor. The cupboard was built using traditional construction and finishing techniques. Photo by Michael Gordon.

If you were trying to recapture the feeling of a typical Colonial American parlor, the first piece of furniture you might want to consider placing in that room might be a built-in: a traditional cockleshell corner cabinet. When Paul Nuckols, of Springfield, Massachusetts, was asked to contribute to one such project, he began by carefully studying the interiors of Connecticut River Valley homes of the 1750s. With the design approval of his corner cupboard secured from his clients, Nuckols began construction, sticking close to traditional materials and techniques. He made up the shelves from 18-in.-wide pine planks and formed the concave-shaped back of 5/4 stock, cutting shiplap joints and hollowing each board so they would form a smooth curve when joined together. He shaped the cockleshell with hand tools from a lamination of pine planks.

Finally, Nuckols selected a paint scheme and shelf configuration to highlight his client's antique creamware collection. (A bit surprisingly from this century's vantage point, a painted cabinet was considered in the Colonial era to be a symbol of wealth—paint was very expensive, and many colonists, especially in the earliest portion of the period, made do with unfinished cabinetry.) The finished cabinet is shown in the photo at left.

What happens, though, when 18th-century design sensibilities encounter 20th-century realities? Cabinetmaker Rex Alexander, of Brethren, Michigan, found out when he was faced with the challenge of building a traditionally inspired chinaware corner cupboard in the corner of a room edged with hot-water heating units. The heating units couldn't be moved, and the cabinet really had to be in this corner. So he had to incorporate the heaters in the design.

As you can see in the photo below left, Alexander's cabinet draws clearly on traditional design elements (such as arched glazed doors and cornice molding) yet includes vents for the heating units that are not only clean and effective, but detract little from the appearance. Alexander does not, in fact, shy away from the shadow line/heat vents in the plinth. Instead, he incorporates them into the design by visually linking them to the rest of the cabinet—notice how the bullnose at the top horizontal line of sash on the doors relates to the nosing just above the upper heater vent.

To cover the heating units on either side of the cabinet, Alexander built slip-on covers in matching wood, orienting the vent openings to those in the corner cabinet. Dovetailed corners relate the covers to the level of craftsmanship in the corner cupboard. As another acknowledgment to the 20th century, Alexander finished the oak cabinets with a hard, clear finish—something rarely seen in traditional 18th-century parlor cabinetwork.

In the course of designing the custom cabinetwork of a new kitchen, I had occasion to create a built-in hutch. Little more than an afterthought to the original kitchen layout, the tiny combination hutch and pantry unit (see the photo below right) found its way into the corridor wall between the kitchen and the dining room. The design was a response to my clients' need for just a bit more pantry shelving for canned goods, and for display space to show off a small

Left: A corner cabinet by Rex Alexander combines a traditional appearance with a modern design consideration: the incorporation of heating-unit vents. Photo by Rex Alexander.

Right: A mini-pantry/china hutch by Jim Tolpin is built into a short length of wall separating a kitchen and dining room. The lower doors conceal adjustable shelves stacked with canned goods. Photo by Jim Tolpin.

This china hutch, built by Galen Marrs of clear vertical-grain fir with spalted maple door panels, gracefully fills an alcove set into the corridor between a kitchen and a dining room. Photo by Craig Wester.

collection of china. Using a scrollsaw fit with a thin blade, I made cutouts in the arched top rails to resemble the California poppy—a plant that grows in abundance in the fields around their house.

The unit was surprisingly easy to build and install. I began by removing sections of the 2x4 wall studs and then framing an opening 1 in. wider and higher than the outside dimensions of the cabinet. Since this was not a load-bearing wall, there was no need to install a header. (Had we thought of it, however, we would have had the contractor frame this wall with 2x6 studs to allow us to increase the depth, and thus the capacity, of the cabinet.) I cut, assembled, and prefinished the casework and doors in my shop, prehanging the doors to adjust their fit. Then, with the doors removed, I slid the unit into the framed opening and inserted shims to level and snug it in place. I secured the case to the studs by screwing from inside the cabinet sides through the shims and into the studs. Finally, I covered the margin around the case with oak quarter-round.

The furnishing shown in the photo at left and built by Galen Marrs, of Port Townsend, Washington, is another example of a china hutch that takes good advantage of a passage between a kitchen and a dining room. The china can be reached—and enjoyed—by people in either space. By carefully scribing the stiles to the sides of the alcove, Marrs avoided using moldings to hide gaps. Free of excess moldings, the hutch remains clean and straightforward, allowing the clear vertical-grain fir, spalted maple panels, and hand-carved handles to articulate the design. In the one place where molding is used—the cornice—it serves to reference the cabinet to the top line of the passageway. This is an effective way to tie the cabinetwork to the interior structures of the building.

Hutches in a Closet

In remodels that either establish or expand upon a dining area, a closet sometimes comes in handy. In the following examples, an existing closet space was converted to an attractive, functional china hutch that does not impinge on the limited floor space of the dining rooms.

Marv Schupp and Greg March, of London, Ontario, designed and built a hutch for a closet that was built into an exterior wall (see the photo below). To maximize space, they expanded its width from 4 ft. to 5 ft. Because the wall is load-bearing, the expansion required the addition of a wide header across the opening. The casework itself was relatively straightforward. Because he was working alone, Schupp built the unit in six modules (so they would be easy to transport) and then installed them into the opening. Depending on the location, he either covered the case-to-case module joints with moldings or used

This china cabinet of birch plywood and poplar is built into the dining room's former 4-ft.-wide closet. Interior lighting draws attention to heirloom china and crystal ware, while glass shelving allows light to diffuse through the cabinet's interior. The cabinet was designed by Marv Schupp and Greg March. Photo by Michael Jordan.

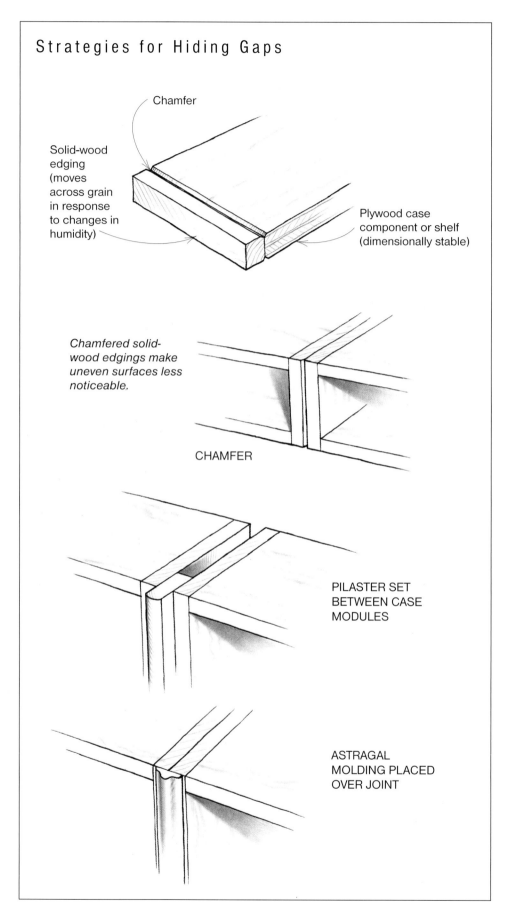

Strategies for Hiding Gaps

Chamfer

Solid-wood edging (moves across grain in response to changes in humidity)

Plywood case component or shelf (dimensionally stable)

Chamfered solid-wood edgings make uneven surfaces less noticeable.

CHAMFER

PILASTER SET BETWEEN CASE MODULES

ASTRAGAL MOLDING PLACED OVER JOINT

shadow lines (chamfers) to conceal inconsistencies (see the drawing at left). Most viewers have no idea that the hutch was constructed of independent sections.

To save money, the two designers used stock moldings to integrate the unit to the room's existing three-piece cornice, chair-rail, and baseboard moldings. The decorative paintwork surrounding the hutch was added later by McCready Painting and Decorating, also of London, Ontario.

The closet that cabinetmaker Rex Alexander, of Brethren, Michigan, was given to work with may have been even more of a challenge than Schupp's bearing-wall situation. Alexander's closet was a recess cut into an existing brick wall for a now-defunct appliance. A cement lintel, decidedly immovable, spanned the opening at a point several feet above the floor. His solution (see the drawing and photo on the facing page) was to make the cabinet in three modules: a glass-doored china hutch and two drawer units. Alexander fit these latter two units above and below the lintel, adding a facing to cover the lintel itself. Vertical edgings on each side tie the stacked modules together, making them appear as a single unit. A triangular molding covers the gap between this edging and the brickwork. A simple, but effective, pin-style lock mechanism provides security for the upper two drawers.

Alexander's China Cupboard

SIDE VIEW

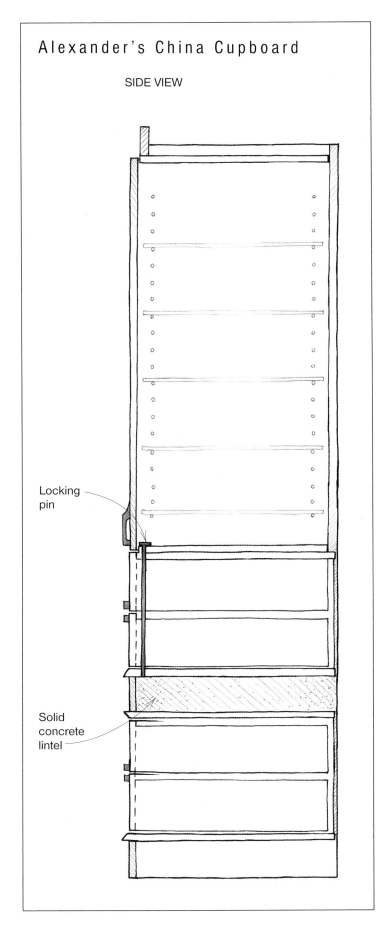

Locking pin

Solid concrete lintel

This china and silverware cupboard in locally grown white birch is recessed into an existing brickwork opening. The horizontal element above the doors mimics the toe inset at the base, elongating the unit visually by emphasizing vertical reference lines. Designed and built by Rex Alexander. Photo by Dietrich Floeter.

A built-in dining settee of solid cherry, designed by Lo-Yi Chan, of New York, N. Y., sweeps elegantly around a raised semicircular kitchen alcove. The dramatic curve of the seat harmonizes comfortably with a multitude of other design elements: the rounded end of the seat board itself, the round dining table and round hanging light, the arced steps to the kitchen area, and the arched back slats of the freestanding chairs.. Photo © Brian Vanden Brink.

Breakfast Nooks and Eating Bars

In every formal dining room that I have seen, the table and chairs have been stand-alone furniture. Situated as they are in the center of the room, there is little option for a built-in alternative. But in less formal settings such as breakfast nooks or eating bars, the table and seats are often built-in furnishings.

In a window alcove located between a kitchen and formal dining room, architect John Silverio, of Lincolnville, Maine, created an eating nook with the addition of a Shaker-inspired trestle table and fixed bench seating (see the photo below). Note that the floor brace of the trestle end has been eliminated: Since the table is secured at one end to the wall, the brace is not needed for stability—its absence makes it easier for people to slip in and out of the seats. Bathed in natural light, situated close to the action in the kitchen yet snugly out of the traffic patterns, the nook has probably seen more meals than the formal dining room just beyond it.

John Silverio's traditional trestle table with built-in bench seating lends elegant simplicity to a Maine cottage. The furnishing was built by John Gertner, Lyle Dennett, and Phil Divinski. Photo © Brian Vanden Brink.

Dan Kagay's wall-hung eating table under a kitchen pass-through also serves as a buffet sideboard for the dining room. Photo by Dan Kagay.

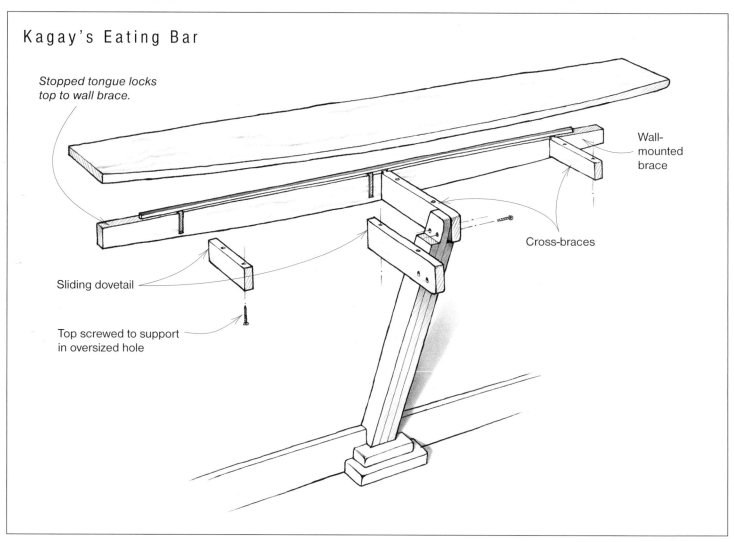

Kagay's Eating Bar

Stopped tongue locks top to wall brace.

Wall-mounted brace

Cross-braces

Sliding dovetail

Top screwed to support in oversized hole

Dan Kagay, of Austin, Texas, located an eating bar—dubbed the "culinary altar"—along the wall pierced by the large kitchen pass-through (see the photo on the facing page). Sitting at the bar, one can have lunch and pester or entertain the cook at the same time. Purposely made narrow to minimize its intrusion into the formal dining room and to keep its seated occupants close to the wall and out of house traffic patterns, the bar serves equally well as an informal lunch counter or as a buffet sideboard.

To support the bar with as uncluttered a system as possible, Kagay designed and installed a single vertical angle brace accompanied by a wall-mounted, lengthwise brace (see the drawing on the facing page). The sliding dovetails that join the cross-braces to the wall brace ensure a strong mechanical connection independent of glue or fasteners. To keep the counter board tight to the wall, Kagay cut a stopped tongue along the wall brace to seat in a groove running on the board's underside. Because the solid wood counter might shrink or expand with seasonal changes in humidity, Kagay attached the cross-braces to the bar top with screws run through oversized holes.

Similar in function, though not in style, to Kagay's built-in is the eating bar designed by John Silverio for a window alcove at the border of a formal dining room (see the photo at right). Though the design looks simple at first glance—and it is refreshingly unpretentious—the attention to detail is remarkable. To create a visual link between this furnishing and the architecture, the openings of the flanking cupboards (which double as supports for the shelf) match the sash proportions of the alcove's bay windows. Meanwhile, the decorative cutout along the bottom edge of the under-counter apron provides knee space and hints at the angular styling of the stool.

John Silverio's plank-shelf eating bar, supported by a pair of open-shelf cupboards, fills a window alcove bordering a formal dining room. The furnishing was built by John Winster, Bruce Lovely, Carl Richardson, and Dick Tyler. Photo © Brian Vanden Brink.

Floor-to-ceiling cabinetry and a large island serve to differentiate the kitchen from the dining and living areas of an open great room. The semicircular bar that juts out from the end of the island keeps kibitzers near the cook, yet out from underfoot. Designed by D. Ralph Katz and built by Timberline Cabinets, Inc., of Cranbury, N. J. Photo by Bill Blanchard Photography.

6
KITCHENS

Fill a space with a sweeping array of built-in furnishings—floor-to-ceiling cabinetry with peninsulas and islands topped with expansive work surfaces—and you have the typical contemporary kitchen: efficient and comfortable to use, easy to clean, and pleasing to look at. People spend a lot of time in the kitchen and demand a lot of this space. We all want a lot of storage room, with easy access to much of it; we want abundant work surfaces oriented to the major appliances, along with lots of open space; we want the kitchen to be cozy, yet not feel cut off from the rest of the home. In addition to basic food-preparation areas, people also want kitchens to include everything from specialized baking centers to a computer station. It's fertile ground indeed for carefully designed and well-made built-in furnishings.

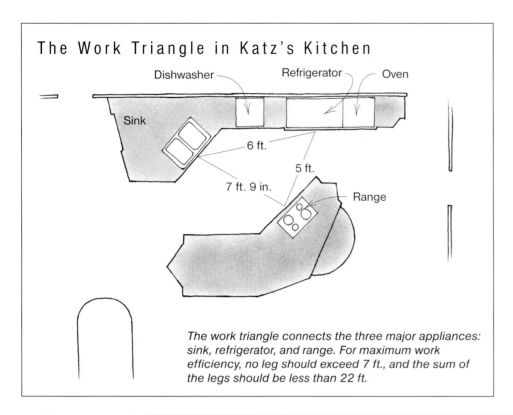

The Work Triangle in Katz's Kitchen

Dishwasher   Refrigerator   Oven

Sink

6 ft.

5 ft.

7 ft. 9 in.

Range

The work triangle connects the three major appliances: sink, refrigerator, and range. For maximum work efficiency, no leg should exceed 7 ft., and the sum of the legs should be less than 22 ft.

One of the most essential ingredients to the creation of a successful kitchen is careful attention to the layout of the major appliances and intervening work surfaces. In one kitchen design by architect D. Ralph Katz (see the photo on p. 84 and the drawing at left), the three most commonly used appliances—the sink, refrigerator, and range—are fairly close together. The cook travels from one to the other within a simple, unobstructed triangle. Research has clearly shown that kitchens lose efficiency when the sum of a work triangle's legs exceeds 22 ft. (and when one leg exceeds 7 ft.). Safety concerns influence the kitchen layout as well: For example, at least 12 in. of counter to either side of the range and at least 3 ft.

A tiny, but efficient, apartment kitchen by Rob Whitten nestles into a half-wall cubby-like space. Notice how the crisp, blocky styling of the cabinetry melds with the square column and rectangular openings. Photo © Brian Vanden Brink.

Edwin Lundii's kitchen in a closet. Photo by Scott Gibson.

of unobstructed space in front of the oven are recommended.

A kitchen does not have to be large to be efficient or a pleasure to work in. The tiny kitchen shown in the photo on the facing page was installed within a 75-sq.-ft. cubicle framed into the corner of a small apartment. In this kitchen, designed by architect Rob Whitten, of Portland, Maine, and built by Shearwater Construction, also of Portland, the major appliances are two to three steps away

from one another and are surrounded by counters for food preparation —it's an ideal arrangement for one cook. The half-walls of the cubicle, terminating in a single column support at the corner, allow light to flow in and out of the space and help connect the kitchen with the rest of the apartment.

How small can you go? Try this: a whole kitchen within a cabinet. Created by designer Edwin Lundii 50 years ago for a cabin in a Minnesota forest, the

kitchen shown in the photo above is little more than a base unit accompanied by open shelving and set behind bifold doors. Inspired by Norwegian architecture, the decoratively pierced doors hang on hand-forged strap hinges. Dishes are stored on a rack on the outside of the "closet" cabinet.

Carefully crafted
and finely detailed
built-in fixtures
by Louis Mackall
create an elegant
alcove around the
kitchen sink. The
columns are poplar,
staved and turned.
The birdhouses
above the columns
are real—though not
presently inhabited!
Photo by Louis
Mackall.

The Kitchen as a Design Statement

Kitchen built-ins must be efficient and safe, but that does not mean they have to be boring. Quite the opposite is true: Kitchen cabinetry offers you the opportunity to create a strong visual statement.

In one bold and beautiful example, shown in the photo on the facing page, architect Louis Mackall, of Guilford, Connecticut, used cabinetry and an arched soffit to sculpt an elegant alcove around a sink and dishwasher. (Though the soffit's arch curves only in one direction—upward—it appears to bow outward into the room as well—a desirable illusion that cost the client nothing!) Three design elements—the columns at the corners of the flanking cabinets; the visual reference line that runs at the level of the window sill and through the cabinetry, and the subtle angle of the flanking cabinets toward the sink—help carry the eye smoothly along the run of cabinets and across the windows. These built-ins do not just fill a space, they clearly create one. The furnishing was built by Breakfast Woodworks, also of Guilford.

The antithesis of the contemporary styling demonstrated by Katz and Mackall, designer Kathleen Vanden Brink's own kitchen, shown in the photo below, was designed around a post-World War II enameled-steel sink cabinet. The colored tiles set above the sink speak joyfully to the 1950s Lu-Ray china collection set out on the open shelving while a vinyl and steel dining set complete the post-war ambience. A window seat of simple, straightforward lines is a comfortable place to sit while chatting with the cook. The kitchen was built by Bill Sideris.

A kitchen rich with the fruits of skillful woodworking emerged from the hands of Dan Kagay of Austin, Texas.

This kitchen, designed by Kathleen Vanden Brink, harks back to the 1950s with its metal cabinets, open shelving, and colorful dishes. Photo © Brian Vanden Brink.

In Dan Kagay's Craftsman-influenced maple cabinetwork, upper cabinets appear to be hung from the soffit with wedged brackets. Note the cubbies for wine bottles. Design collaboration with Rick and Laura Brown of Brookline, Mass. Photos by Rick Brown.

In this kitchen (see the photo at left), the inset, strictly rectilinear doors, hand-forged iron hardware, exaggerated "proud" joinery of the drawer faces, and the iron-wedged brackets are all reminiscent of Craftsman-era casework. As shown in the photo and drawing below, the "hanging" brackets are essentially aesthetic—the upper cabinets are actually secured to the wall.

Weinstein Copeland Architects, of Seattle, Washington, designed a kitchen to complement the sleek interior architecture of a contemporary lake-front home. The cabinets (see the photos on the facing page) are faced with slab-style doors and drawer fronts. With hard maple veneered to a hardwood-plywood substrate, they are light colored and highly resistant to abuse. The base units are composed entirely of drawers—that's what the cook prefers. Windows between the lower and upper case units bring natural light across the work surfaces.

Kagay's Hanging Bracket

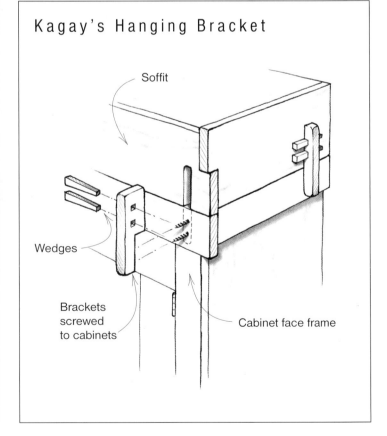

Soffit

Wedges

Brackets screwed to cabinets

Cabinet face frame

In this all-maple kitchen, designed by Weinstein Copeland Architects, the dining table (designed and built by Bill Walker) can be repositioned to serve as a buffet. Photos by Craig Wester.

At the far end of the kitchen, a large L-shaped window seat lets dinner guests relax before and after the meal. Photo by Craig Wester.

The dramatic moldings and columns of this peninsula counter by Richard Mincey firmly establish this kitchen in the Southern neoclassical style. Photo by Doug Gilmore.

Blending with Moldings

Most modern kitchens are not expected to stand on their own architecturally. Instead, their designers strive to blend the cabinetry into the overall scheme of the home's interior woodwork. The obvious way to do this is to match the construction materials and the styling of the doors, end panels and drawer faces to these details appearing elsewhere in the house—or at least to those in the adjoining room.

To anchor the built-ins to the existing interior work, the designer may ask the cabinetmaker to install moldings that match those running through the rest of the room. In the example shown in the photo above, cabinetmaker Richard Mincey, of Lexington, South Carolina, continued the multi-layered cornice molding around the soffits to which the upper casework is attached. The fluted columns supporting the peninsula soffit add to the Southern neoclassical design scheme.

Careful attention to the design and execution of the trimwork meld this kitchen's open shelf casework, designed by Louis Mackall, into and around the passage door and built-in bookcase. Photos by Louis Mackall.

The extensive open-shelf casework of a kitchen designed by Louis Mackall, of Guilford, Connecticut, and built by Breakfast Woodworks, also of Guilford, provided an opportunity to extend matching trim around the passage door and into the living area (where the open shelving continues as a bookcase). In this kitchen (see the photos above and at right), Mackall ran the trim around the door at an angle—without this chamfer the door would look abruptly boxed in, constricted, and visually jarring.

Take note of the careful attention given to the molding details: The beaded inside edges of the stiles recalls the larger bead defining the perimeter of the door trim. Shelf edges are bullnosed and are allowed to ride on the face of the stiles to create a more visually dramatic effect. Finally, the lowest shelf is buttressed by an angled molding, which lends strength and visual weight to the shelf, hides lighting behind, and links it architecturally to the chamfered door trim.

From commercial storage fixtures to clever shop-made solutions to simple shelving strategies, a designer has a wealth of options for maximizing the efficiency and economy of a kitchen's built-in cabinetwork. On these four pages you'll get a glimpse of some examples.

Left: A sink base unit, designed and built by Tom Simmons, of Santa Barbara, California, makes exceptionally good use of commercial storage fixtures: a spice drawer, a pullout cutting board, a tilt sink front, an extending towel bar, and roll-out shelving. These fixtures usually install easily with minimum modification to the cabinetwork. Photo by Tom Simmons.

Below: A pair of unusual appliance garages, built by cabinetmaker John Marckworth, of Port Townsend, Washington. In each, the bottom shelf extends out on full-extension slides and is enclosed behind flip-up doors when not in use. In the version at left, adjustable shelves are set behind bifold doors; in the version at right, pocket doors enclose a slide-out shelf. Photos by Craig Wester.

To avoid awkwardly narrow wall cabinets between windows, certified kitchen designer Tom Trzcinski, of Kitchen & Bath Concepts, Pittsburgh, Pennsylvania, substituted a long run of appliance garages. To accommodate them, Trzcinski pulled the base cabinets away from the wall 12 in. The bubinga-faced cabinets between the flip-up door garages make a dramatic and rich visual statement and tie in with other bubinga elements. Design collaboration with John Petrus. Cabinets by Neff Kitchen Manufacturing of Toronto, Canada. Photo by Wayne Simco.

In a home built by Ravenhill Construction, of Friday Harbor, Washington, designer Tom Bosworth, of Seattle, Washington, specified that shelves be run across the bank of windows—note that they coincide with the lines of horizontal sash. To avoid vertical shelf supports (which would block light), the cabinetmakers buried steel L-brackets behind the window trim and inside the shelf sandwich. Downlighting units hidden in white painted canisters look like jars sitting on the shelf (look for one just above the sink faucet). Photo by Craig Wester.

The cookbook shelf in an upper cabinet unit, designed by Lou Ekus and built by Henry Walas of Belchertown, Massachusetts, swings out to reveal storage for pots and pans. The side of the pivoting case had to be angled to allow swinging clearance. The metal rod with turnbuckle resists compression, helping prevent the case from sagging. Photos © Brian Vanden Brink.

In this kitchen, cabinetmaker Keith Evans, of Canonsburg, Pennsylvania, managed to hide a miniature office behind the bifold doors of an angled corner cabinet. The desk is configured so that the swivel chair can also be enclosed when not in use. Photo by Steve Burchesky.

Kitchen China Cabinets

Though more commonly placed in the dining room, display cabinets for china also find their way into the modern kitchen, usually near the dining-room entrance. Their presence within the kitchen is much appreciated by the cook/dishwasher: The dishes are easier to replace after washing and, arranged decorously behind glass doors, their beauty is more readily appreciated. After all, where do cooks spend most of their time?

Cabinetmaker Grady Matthews of Brier, Washington, took advantage of the last section in a run of floor-to-ceiling cabinets to design and build a tall china cupboard by the dining-room passage door (see the photo below). Glass installed in both the doors and end panels allow the contents to be viewed from anywhere in the kitchen.

Architect Andy Neumann, of Carpinteria, California, surrounded the pass-through between a kitchen and dining room with flanking glass-doored cabinets, joining them together structurally as well as visually with a simple cornice molding and frieze board. The effect (see the photo at left on the facing page) is reminiscent of a

This kitchen by Grady Matthews features a china cabinet built into a run of floor-to-ceiling cherry cabinet units. Note the elegant ebony door pulls and unusual mitered door frames. Photo by Grady Matthews.

traditional freestanding hutch. Note the efficiency of this design: With the dishwasher nearby, clean glasses can easily be put away; those destined for a formal meal can be set on the tile counter of the pass-through—a step or two away from the dining table. The hutch was built by John Willis.

Ned Forrest Architects, of Sonoma, California, designed a china cupboard that defines the boundary between the kitchen proper and the "scullery" extending into an alcove. The back of the unit is filled with deep shelving that opens to the rear. On the front of the unit (see the photo below right), the serpentine marble counter, leaded-glass door panes and the magnificent molding details, by Dean Coley of Watsonville, California, firmly root the cabinet in the 19th-century English period style of the rest of the home.

The hutch-like cabinet unit of Andy Neumann's kitchen provides convenient storage for glassware and a pass-through to the dining room. Photo by Bill Zeldis.

A built-in china hutch by Ned Forrest Architects doubles as an island that defines the boundary between the kitchen and the scullery. Photo by Sandor Nagyszalanczy.

This mudroom pantry matches the 1739 architecture in the rest of the house. The one concession to progress is the running water at the sink for washing garden vegetables. Designed by Jane Langmuir of Providence, R. I., and built by Steve Tyson of the Architectural Preservation Group, Apanaug R. I. Photo © Brian Vanden Brink.

Kitchen Pantries

One distinct advantage of a pantry with built-in shelving and cupboards has gone unchanged over the centuries: A pantry alleviates the need for extensive cabinetwork in the kitchen. In Colonial America, cabinetwork (which was freestanding furniture back then) was expensive and hard to come by. Today, a good-sized pantry can all but eliminate the need for wall-hung cabinets—not only saving money but also allowing more light, and with it a sense of spaciousness, to enter the room.

Today, a pantry isn't necessarily located in a room separate from the kitchen. Cabinetmakers now create pantry-like storage within a floor-to-ceiling cabinet unit. In the example shown in the photo at right, Tom Simmons and Mike Roberts, of Santa Barbara, California, built storage systems in two layers. To the back of the unit are shelves (some are height-adjustable) and slide-out bins. In front of these are a pair of swing-out shelf units designed to hold canned goods. Cross rods—hardwood dowels—prevent the contents from spilling out when the units are opened and closed. The cabinet can store a huge inventory of foodstuffs, yet presents a clean, crisp appearance to the kitchen when closed behind a pair of doors made from hardwood plywood panels edged with strips of solid wood.

A floor-to-ceiling cabinet unit becomes a pantry when outfitted with adjustable shelves, slide-out bins, and shop-made, swing-out shelf units. Photo by Tom Simmons.

To make the most of limited space, Peter Kilpatrick's partition wall separating the kitchen entry from the living room is faced with pantry storage shelving. All the shelves except for the one at the middle are height-adjustable. Photo by Craig Wester.

Peter Kilpatrick, of Friday Harbor, Washington, took a different approach. The "pantry" he designed (it was built by Ravenhill Construction) is little more than a stack of shelves (made from ¾-in. plywood with 1½-in. high wood edging for strength) built against the partition wall separating the kitchen entry from the living room of a tiny cottage (see the photo at left). The shelves provide enough storage to eliminate wall cupboards, and they are ideally located: When groceries are carried in through this entry, they are placed on the counter directly opposite the pantry and next to the refrigerator. Putting them away thus requires only a single step.

Today's pantries may be asked to contain some things that would never have been seen in the pantries of Colonial America—things like recycling bins, not to mention electrical appliances. In a pantry/cabinet unit designed and built by Mike Nolin of Brewster, Massachusetts, there are both. As you can see in the photo on the facing page, a typical array of modern appliances sits behind a long tambour door, instantly accessible when needed. Just below, eight pull-out bins—sized to hold a standard paper shopping bag and clearly labeled—separate recyclables. The tall doors to either side of the appliance garage pull out on full-extension slides, drawing with them shelves that store canned goods.

Mike Nolin's massive cherry pantry/recycling center occupies one wall of a remodeled kitchen. A long tambour door conceals the appliances, and slide-out compartments below, lined with paper bags, serve as recycling bins. Photo by Todd Goodrich.

7
ROOMS FOR READING
AND ENTERTAINMENT

Behold the classic library: built-in shelves for books that, interspersed with cabinets for storing documents and fragile tomes, wrap the perimeter of the room and embrace a comfortable reading chair. The shelves do not function or appear to stand as independent units—indeed, they are the walls of the room. Filled with books and artifacts, these built-in furnishings imbue the space with an ambience of collected wisdom and quiet contemplation. They welcome you into a place where you will be entertained and educated by books.

It is certainly a lot easier on designers and builders when all a furnishing has to do is hold books on a shelf or inside a cabinet. After all, books are easy to accommodate: They are compact, predictably uniform in dimension, easily removable, and best of all, they don't

A library in American Neoclassical style, designed in 1858 by Boston architect Harvey Graves. Photo © Brian Vanden Brink.

A contemporary classic library shelving system in solid walnut, designed by Dave Lehman. Photo by Steve Echols.

Tom Bosworth designed these built-in furnishings of painted plywood for a library in a step-down alcove to one side of a great room. Photo by Craig Wester.

need to be plugged in. But as you will see later in this chapter, a contemporary "library" may need to contain not only books, but also state-of-the-art audio and visual equipment. It must also incorporate up-to-date lighting, wiring, and heating.

Libraries

In a contemporary version of the classic library, designer Dave Lehman, of Goshen, Indiana, filled an entire room with built-in bookshelves, cupboards, and framed raised panels of solid walnut (see the photo above). Since he specified that no stain be added to the wood, the builders, Swartzendruber Hardwood Creations, also of Goshen, carefully selected each board for color and figure. Solid brass hardware—butt hinges and pulls—add to the elegance. As a concession to modern times, Lehman incorporated heating ducts in the toe kicks and top boards.

To create a well-defined and cozy, yet easily accessible space, architect Tom Bosworth, of Seattle, Washington, situated the library of a contemporary home in an alcove two steps below the level of the central great room (see the bottom photo on the facing page). While a traditional library is commonly set off from the rest of the home (and built mainly of rich-colored woods), Bosworth chose to make this room highly visible. The lack of moldings, the crisp rectilinear lines, and the white painted plywood meld the room with the interior architecture of the great room. A couch in the bay window area—barely visible in the photo—is a comfortable place to read. A wealth of natural light illuminates the room by day, while carefully placed reading lamps fill the alcove with a soft amber glow at night. The lights provide adequate light for reading without over-illuminating the rest of the library, destroying the cozy nighttime ambience. The library was built by Dan Paulson of Friday Harbor, Washington, with casework by Boothman Cabinets, also of Friday Harbor.

A very different style of library is shown in the photo at right. The clients wanted a "library in a forest cathedral." So the architects, Mark Simon and Marriette Hines Gomez, of Centerbrook Architects, Essex, Connecticut, gave it to them, filling the three-story-high arched ceiling with "branches" springing from the tops of natural cedar posts—Gothic au naturel. Comfortable leather sofas fill the room, placed back to back against tables that can hold reading lamps, plants, and art objects. An immense, steeply gabled fireplace adds to the Gothic feel of the space and to the sense of height. In the photo, you can see the ladder used for accessing the top display shelves. Like the posts, it is made from raw timber.

This reading room, designed by Mark Simon and Marriette Hines Gomez, was inspired by the great halls of medieval Europe. Books and magazines set in public-library-like display shelves line the walls. Photo by Norman McGrath.

Where is the full-size passage door to the hallway that runs behind Ivan Stancioff's library? It's to the right of the fireplace, behind the fake books on the fake shelves. Photo © Brian Vanden Brink.

SECRET DOORS

What would a traditional library be without a secret room or passageway sequestered behind a massive bookcase? Certainly not as much fun. Though not as common as we would like to imagine, some Early American libraries did have a concealed passageway to another part of the house—an ideal way to get away from visiting relatives. Mostly, however, the secret spaces provided additional storage for valuable books and documents. The challenge for cabinetmakers then, as it is today, was to camouflage a movable case to make it indistinguishable from the surrounding shelves, and they came up with several clever solutions: A bookcase might swing from a hinge like a door, pivot around a center point, or slide into a flanking wall like a huge pocket door.

If you look carefully at the top photo on the facing page, you will notice that the shelves to the right side of the fireplace lack depth—in fact they are only strips of wood glued to an oak plywood panel. The books are, of course, fake as well. Obtained from Bernard Weaver of London, England, the 1/2-in.-deep "books" are actually hand-painted plastic-resin castings.

To camouflage the passageway (which leads to an entry hallway), Ivan Stancioff, of Lincolnville, Maine, applied the woodwork and castings to a sheet of oak plywood, which he then fastened to the face of a standard six-panel passage door (see the drawing at right). To ensure that the door would not sag under the extra weight, he upgraded the butt hinges to ball-bearing versions and attached them with extra-long screws into the studs framing the door opening. While there is a doorknob installed on the passageway side, it cannot open the door unless its latch is electrically activated by pressing a button concealed in a bookcase that runs along the side wall.

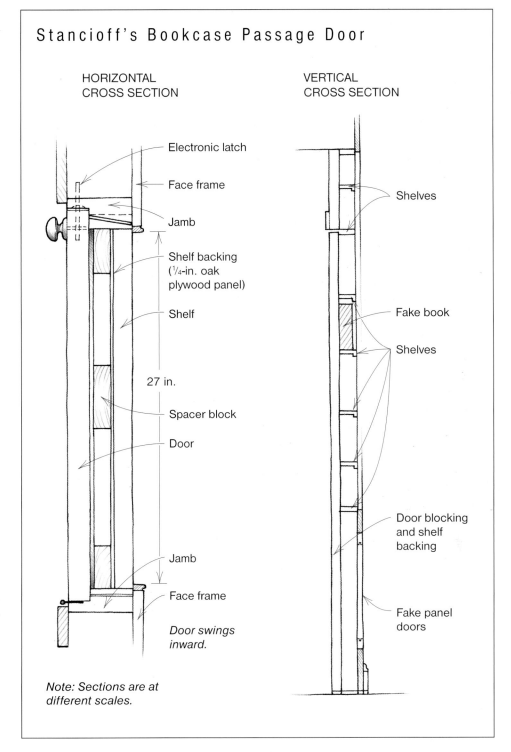

Stancioff's Bookcase Passage Door

HORIZONTAL CROSS SECTION

VERTICAL CROSS SECTION

Electronic latch

Face frame

Jamb

Shelf backing (1/4-in. oak plywood panel)

Shelf

27 in.

Spacer block

Door

Jamb

Face frame

Door swings inward.

Note: Sections are at different scales.

Shelves

Fake book

Shelves

Door blocking and shelf backing

Fake panel doors

Above: In this library designed by Ned Forrest, tight-fitting moldings at the top, counter, and baseboard mesh tightly together, concealing the fact that the large section of the bookcase to the left pivots open to reveal a document storage room. Facing page: Builder Dean Coley swings open the 1,500-lb. section of bookcase. Photos by Sandor Nagyszalanczy.

The secret door in a library designed by Ned Forrest of Sonoma, California, took me a long time to discover (see the photo on the facing page). Once I did, I found it hard to believe how little effort it took to pivot this three-quarter-ton bookcase open and closed (see the photo below). And because the case swivels wobble-free on its steel shaft (see the drawing at right), the coped moldings at the top, counter, and baseboard mesh tightly together each time the unit swings shut— the camouflage is perfect. Because the entire weight of the case rests on a single point, builder Dean Coley, of Watsonville, California, beefed up the joists in this area to prevent any sagging or deflection of the floor. Note the sliding ladder: though shop-built, it features commercial rollers and a rail system to ensure smooth, safe, and trouble-free operation.

Coley's Bookcase Pivot Hardware (Side View)

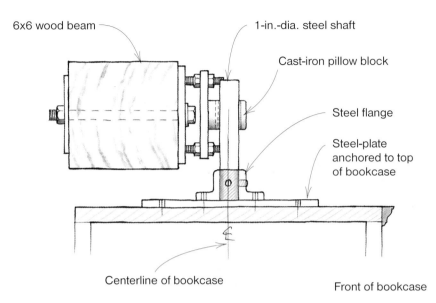

TOP PIVOT

6x6 wood beam

1-in.-dia. steel shaft

Cast-iron pillow block

Steel flange

Steel-plate anchored to top of bookcase

Centerline of bookcase

Front of bookcase

Note: Top pivot shaft must be square and plumb to bookcase at center point.

BOTTOM PIVOT

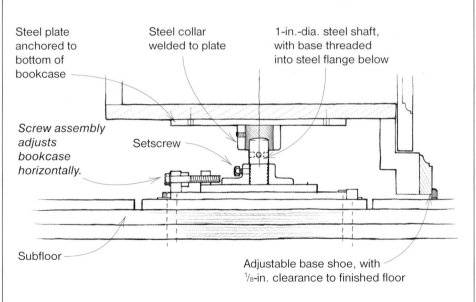

Steel plate anchored to bottom of bookcase

Steel collar welded to plate

1-in.-dia. steel shaft, with base threaded into steel flange below

Screw assembly adjusts bookcase horizontally.

Setscrew

Subfloor

Adjustable base shoe, with 1/8-in. clearance to finished floor

Note: Meeting surfaces of three bottom plates must be finished smooth and greased to allow free movement while adjusting.

In this bookshelf system, designed by Cliff Friedlander and Howard Rudermanof, one "wall" is in fact a pair of pocket doors that can slide open to allow passage into an adjoining room. Photo by Cliff Friedlander.

For a third solution to the concealment problem, look at the photos on the facing page. Rather than pivoting or swinging open, these contemporary-styled bookcases surprise you by separating and disappearing into the flanking walls. The hardware and guide systems that provide the sliding action are surprisingly simple: Moldings guide the bookcases at the top while a wood runner strip keeps the cases on track at the bottom (see the drawing at right). To allow the cases to slide easily and smoothly, Cliff Friedlander and Howard Rudermanof, of Santa Cruz, California, installed heavy-duty skateboard wheels. A distinct advantage to this system over a pivot or hinged system is that the cases can disappear into the walls. Opening the units creates a wide, unobstructed passageway between the two rooms, dramatically enlarging them.

MINI-LIBRARIES

In the classic library, book shelving runs along the walls of a room from floor to ceiling. Often, however, designers are called upon not to create an entire library room, but to take advantage of a certain space or existing cabinetry to provide whatever book shelving they can—in effect, a mini-library. For example, architect Louis Mackall, of Guilford, Connecticut, used the back side of a large kitchen-island structure to provide a home for books that would face the sitting area (see the photo on p. 114). The refined bullnosed edges and rich cherry wood of the shelves lend formality and create a dramatic contrast to the white painted cabinetry. Notice that the front edge of the shelves curves gently outward, increasing both the physical and visual depth of the unit.

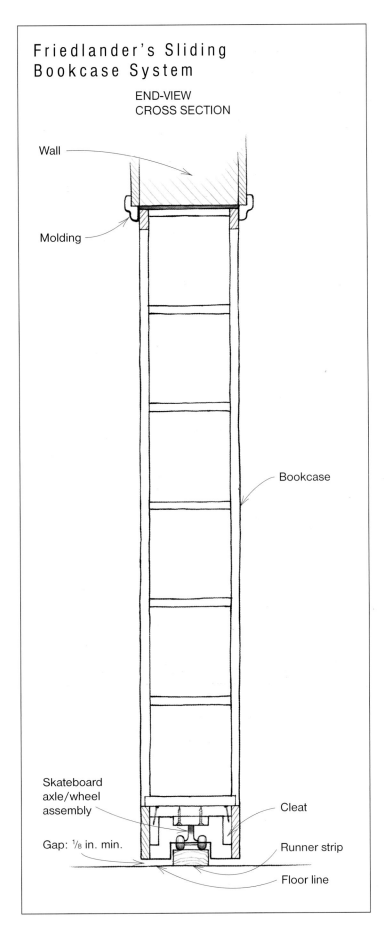

Friedlander's Sliding Bookcase System

END-VIEW CROSS SECTION

Wall

Molding

Bookcase

Skateboard axle/wheel assembly

Gap: 1/8 in. min.

Cleat

Runner strip

Floor line

Louis Mackall's multipurpose cabinet unit defines a visual and functional boundary between the kitchen area and living space in a house with an open floor plan. Photo © Karen Bussolini.

The unit was built by Breakfast Woodworks, also of Guilford.

In another mini-library (see the photo below), the designer and builder, Alex Spear, of Port Townsend, Washington, took advantage of an existing niche to find space for bookshelves. The small bookshelf unit in clear, vertical-grain fir maximizes the use of the dead space created where a half-wall projects out from a partition near the stairway.

Notice how the subtly curved top apron imbues these simple shelves with an understated elegance.

When David Weisman, of Ann Arbor, Michigan, remodeled his bedroom, he decided to add a small library to the space. After he removed the two existing closets and exposed the stairwell, an unusual but surprisingly suitable space revealed itself: the head room over the stairs. Here Weisman

A diminutive built-in bookshelf by Alex Spear takes full advantage of a space created by a stairway partition wall. Photo by Craig Wester.

By removing a closet and framing a platform over an existing stairwell, David Weisman was able to add a library and "reading room" to a small bedroom. The wood is clear vertical-grain fir. Photo by Golden Photography.

Weisman's Bedroom Remodel

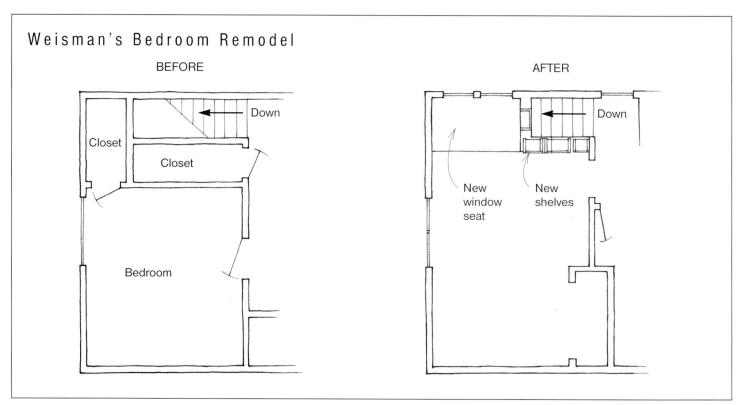

BEFORE

Closet

Closet

Down

Bedroom

AFTER

Down

New window seat

New shelves

installed a pair of south-facing windows and framed a 2x4 platform to create a window seat (which was dimensioned to accept a standard-sized futon). Using 2x8s to frame the platform's support wall and the stairwell's partition wall allowed him to recess the book-shelves (see the drawing on the facing page)—a clever and economical strategy that minimizes the protrusion of the shelving into the bedroom. Drawers under the window seat run the full width of the platform, providing ample storage for bedding.

Cabinetmaker Janice Smith's clients wanted to add a set of bookshelves to their living room without losing access to a pair of closets that dominated one of the walls. Using the closets themselves for shelving was not an option. Smith, of Lawrence, Kansas, solved the problem by surrounding the closets with the shelv-ing (see the photo below). Integrating the moldings and other design elements to make the closets appear to penetrate the shelving ensured that the closets and the shelving would appear as one integrated unit. Notice in the photo how

the cornice molding capping the top of the shelves continues smoothly across the top of the closet molding. Also notice how the half-round trim strips on the door faces relate to the lines of the individual shelves. Uplighting hidden behind the cornice adds soft back-lighting to the room.

Smith cut the radiused ends of the shelves on a bandsaw and then bullnosed their edges with a router. To make the curved faces of the toe kick and upper frieze boards, she glue-laminated six layers of $\frac{1}{8}$-in. bending plywood around

These shelves, designed by Janice Smith, flow around an existing closet. Careful integration of the shelving (which includes a set of glass-enclosed cabinets for rare books) and closet trim makes the structures appear to have been built as a single unit. Photo by Janice Smith.

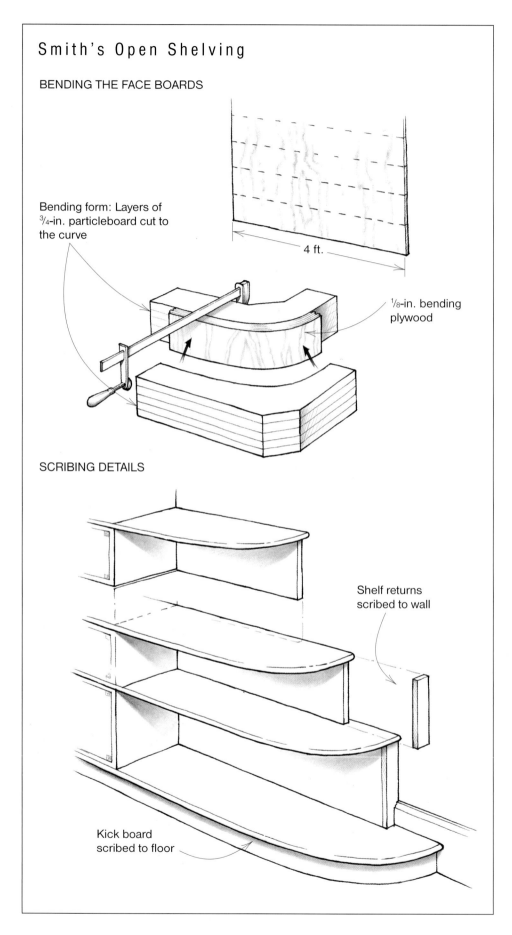

Smith's Open Shelving

BENDING THE FACE BOARDS

4 ft.

Bending form: Layers of ³/₄-in. particleboard cut to the curve

¹/₈-in. bending plywood

SCRIBING DETAILS

Shelf returns scribed to wall

Kick board scribed to floor

a form (see the drawing at left). She bent the plywood across its 4-ft. width to increase its ability to accept the tight radius (about 12 in.).

To ensure that the shelf unit would sit level and would precisely match the top line of the closet door trim, Smith constructed a separate base frame and shimmed it level and to the appropriate height. Then she applied the curved kick board, scribing it to the out-of-level floor. Because the wall behind the shelf unit was neither flat nor plumb, Smith also decided to add scribed returns to the ends of the glass-doored book boxes and to the shelf supports. This strategy allows them to sit plumb, yet fit tightly to the wall surface.

LIBRARY UNITS

Though library shelving units are huge pieces of woodworking, they are not truly architectural built-ins in the strictest sense of the term since they stand independently of the structure that contains them. They are certainly not movable like a chair, but they can be disassembled into modular components and transported to another location. Once reassembled and put in place, they are usually fastened to the wall structure to prevent vibration or collapse should the building tremble from wind, earth-quakes, or rambunctious children.

The library designed and built by Nathaniel Smelser, of Bradenton, Florida, covers nearly 20 lin. ft. of living-room wall space. The unit (see the photo on the facing page) breaks down into 13 pieces, making it possible to ship the library overseas should his clients decide to move it to their European home. Because the ceiling-to-floor measurements were off by more than 1½ in. from one end of the run to the other (and Smelser did not know the

Though it looks monolithic, Nathaniel Smelser's massive shelving unit in solid cherry is actually composed of 13 separate modules. A television set hides behind the corner doors. Photo by Gary Sweetman.

condition of the European home), he decided to support the casework on commercially made adjustable threaded legs. Rather than fitting the cornice molding tightly to the ceiling, Smelser rounded the top profile, allowing a shadow line to form. This design detail allows the piece to sit slightly away from the ceiling, yet not draw attention to an uneven gap line. The rounding also allows the cornice to resolve independently of a surface should the unit someday stand in a room with a high ceiling.

A design collaboration between Seattle sculptor Michael Braden and cabinetmaker Andrew de Klerk, the library shelving unit shown in the photo on p. 122 has a number of unusual features—both aesthetic and structural.

If you are designing shelving, you will have to support it appropriately or it will sag (or possibly even break). How far apart should you space shelf supports to avoid sagging? The answer depends on a number of variables, including the thickness and density of the shelf stock (hardwood won't sag as much as particleboard), the depth of the shelf, the load the shelf must support (use 35 lb. per lin. ft. for library shelves), and the amount of deflection you are willing to allow across the span of the shelving (³⁄₃₂ in. is the amount I generally use). There's an engineering formula for calculating span (you can find it in most texts on structural design), but the graph below, which was generated by Dr. Francis Natali, will tell you what you need to know for five common shelving materials. Of course, if the design requirements of your built-in are out of the ordinary, it's a good idea to have the support system engineered.

If you'd rather not place shelf supports closer together, you can make a shelf stronger by doing one or a combination of the following (see the drawing on the facing page):

Stiffen the shelf by adding ledgers at the front edge; use thicker stock (tapering the front edge for looks, if you want); add a back support ledger or partial partitions; or construct the shelf as a torsion box.

Spans for Common Shelving Materials

This chart assumes a shelf depth of 8 in., a load of 35 lb. per lin. ft., and a maximum allowable deflection between supports of ³⁄₃₂ in.

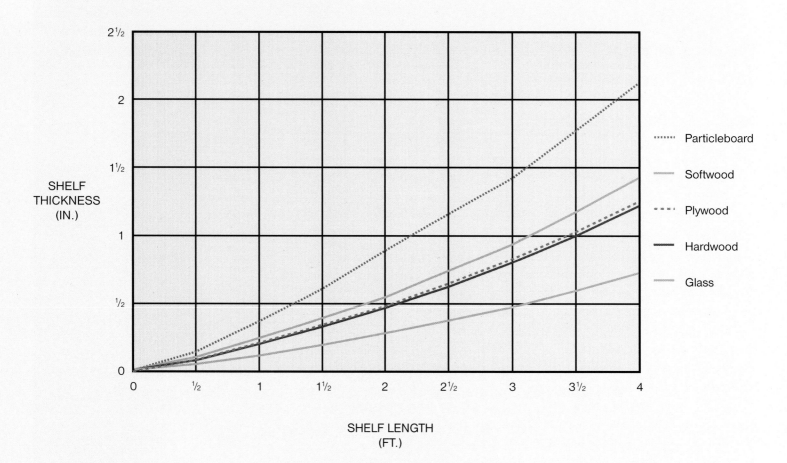

Shelf Stiffening Options

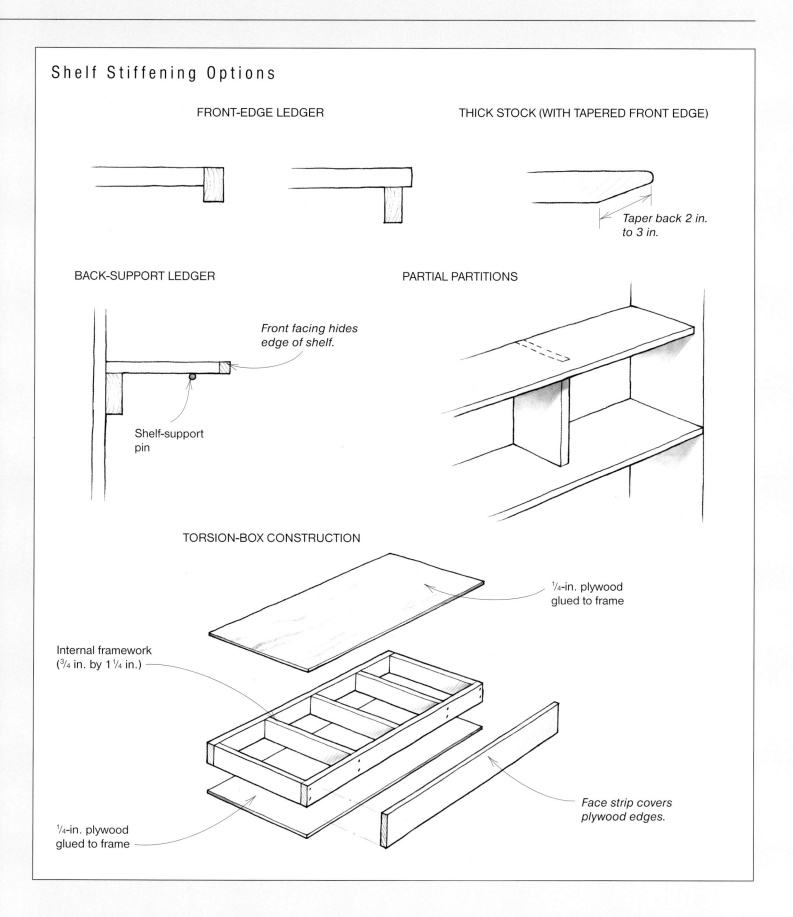

FRONT-EDGE LEDGER

THICK STOCK (WITH TAPERED FRONT EDGE)

Taper back 2 in. to 3 in.

BACK-SUPPORT LEDGER

PARTIAL PARTITIONS

Front facing hides edge of shelf.

Shelf-support pin

TORSION-BOX CONSTRUCTION

$1/4$-in. plywood glued to frame

Internal framework ($3/4$ in. by $1 1/4$ in.)

Face strip covers plywood edges.

$1/4$-in. plywood glued to frame

Unusual patterns and angled edges enliven an artfully designed bookcase system by Michael Braden and Andrew de Klerk. Photo by Craig Wester.

Applying aniline dye to the riftsawn red oak created unusual colors and patterns that lend the piece playfulness and visual excitement within an elegant overall form. The step-back in depth (from 12 in. down to 10 in.) of the two side shelf units has two functions: It adds visual interest by reducing the potentially dull monolithic appearance of this large structure, and it allows space for the room's entry door and a window on the opposite wall.

Like Smelser's unit (see pp. 118-119), de Klerk's version is made up of modular components—in this case, three. Cleverly, Braden and de Klerk designed the stiles that bridge the modules to attach without fasteners—a strategy that allows the moldings to be removed and reinstalled without creating potentially unsightly nail or screw holes. The cabinet bolts draw the module sides tightly together, applying side pressure to the tongue of the pilaster molding, holding it in place. The drawing below shows how it works.

Entertainment Centers

Entertainment centers are a modern offshoot of library built-ins, and they are far more complicated to design and build. Modern media are predominantly electronic—the equipment must be seen and heard from a distance (and well coddled to prevent damage from overheating and vibration. This, then, puts new demands on the makers of the furnishings that must contain them. Not only must designers let the equipment determine some of the basic proportions, but they must also concern themselves with the placement of the unit in the room. Otherwise, the sights and sounds of the equipment may not be suitably projected to the audience.

For example, shelving and cubbies should accommodate changing varieties and models of equipment while allowing easy access to the equipment for maintenance and wiring. A venting system to allow air circulation should be included in the design. Specially sized and compartmentalized drawers are needed for CDs, cassette tapes, videotapes, and laser disks. If speakers are to be mounted in the unit, the designer and builder must be careful to eliminate any potential for vibration. This can be done by avoiding loose components such as adjustable shelves and loose-fitting panels, by installing closing pads on doors and drawer faces, and by fastening the unit securely to the wall. Finally, since many people find electronic gear unattractive to look at, designers often plan ways to hide the stuff when it's not in use. Indeed, it can be quite a challenge to design a fine piece of furniture that contains a wide-screen television set and a huge surround-sound speaker system.

Dan and Sheila Hamilton, of Bluffton, South Carolina, successfully met the challenges of designing an entertainment center with the 8-ft.-high by 12-ft.-wide

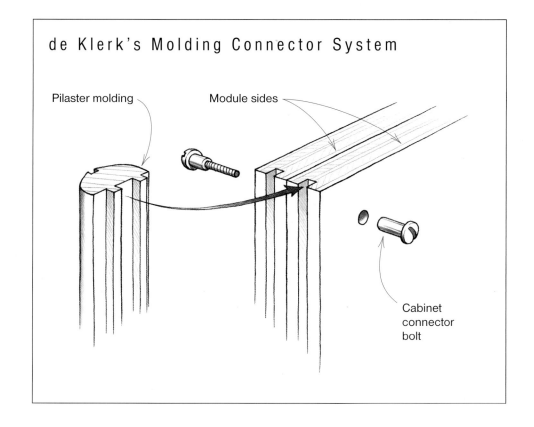

de Klerk's Molding Connector System

Pilaster molding

Module sides

Cabinet connector bolt

This entertainment center by Dan and Sheila Hamilton has several clever features. The columns pull out, drawing out the attached shelving for liquor. Flipper doors hide the television. Mirrors at the back of the glass-doored cabinets give the unit a feeling of depth. Find the secret compartments: the removable panel in the recess over the cupboards and the pull-out toe-kick drawer. Photos by Dustin Peck.

furnishing of solid cherry shown in the photo on the facing page. It's hard to believe that this unit contains a wide-screen television set, a full complement of audiovisual equipment, a speaker system, an extensive collection of videotapes and CDs, books, and a wet bar, along with a sizable stock of spirits and glassware. There are also two hidden compartments, which are visible in the bottom photo if you look carefully.

The secret to this successful design lies in tasteful styling, good proportions, clever storage strategies, and superb craftsmanship. Pay particular attention to the unique pull-out vertical shelves where half-column pilaster moldings (made by lathe-turning a staved octagon round and then slicing it in half) are fastened to the end of a plywood-backed shelf system which is, in turn, mounted to a set of full-extension drawer slides. Also note the hinged columns on either side of the television: These cover the ends of the flipper pocket doors when opened (hiding the rather ugly end view of the pocket-door system) and also increase the size of the compartment to allow room for a larger set. Other flipper doors cover banks of slide-out bins. Where's the speaker system? The center speaker is behind the speaker cloth that covers the back of the "sunburst shell" directly above the television.

When cabinetmaker Barrie Graham, of Arundel, Quebec, was called to design the entertainment center shown in the photo on p. 126, he was faced with a barrage of challenges: The unit had to fit to an irregular masonry wall along one side and to the rear of a firewood box that would protrude 4 in. into its back. The electronic components had to stack on individual full-extension slides (which needed to be adjustable in height to accommodate equipment changes). The equipment would be concealed behind a tambour door—a cooling system would be needed to dissipate the heat. An extensive collection of videotapes needed to be stored in an organized, easy-to-access fashion. Since the center would also accommodate an office system—which would hide when not in

WIRING AN ENTERTAINMENT CENTER

Getting all the wires through a wire chase and to the correct equipment is a difficult task when setting up an entertainment center for the first time. It's even worse, however, when you have to run new wiring for replacement or additional equipment, especially if the chase is already constricted with a mass of existing wiring. One effective method for painlessly running new wiring (courtesy of Barrie Graham, of Arundel, Quebec) is to add a permanent feed cord during the construction of the chase.

As shown in the drawing at right, the feed cord is a nylon cord—knotted or tied around a length of wood to prevent unintentional removal and twice as long as the overall length of the wire chase. To run a new wire, tape one end to the middle of the nylon cord. Then pull the cord through the chase until the new wire comes into the bay of the appropriate component. Then untie and connect the wire, and return the cord to its starting position.

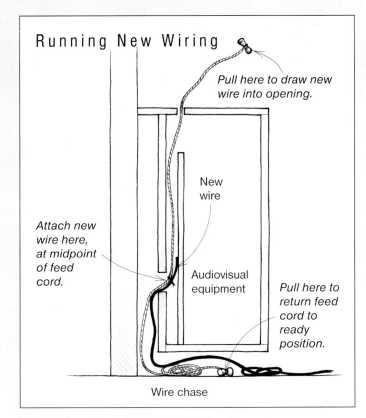

Running New Wiring

Pull here to draw new wire into opening.

New wire

Attach new wire here, at midpoint of feed cord.

Audiovisual equipment

Pull here to return feed cord to ready position.

Wire chase

use—a drop-down desk and file drawers would have to be accommodated as well.

Graham began by designing the case to fit around the protrusions, stepping the back around the firewood box and scribing a trim stile to fit between the masonry and the case side wall. To dissipate heat, Graham ducted air forced from a fan in the basement (to reduce its noise) into the wire chase and up the back of the equipment stack. The fan automatically turns on when triggered by a heat-sensing unit mounted near the top of the stack. Dog-bone-shaped boards behind each shelf allow the air to flow horizontally across each component and then continue upward to escape holes (see the drawing on the facing page). To make the slide-out shelves adjustable in height, Graham riveted the full-extension slides to shop-made hanging clips shaped to fit to a standard shelf-support track.

THE IMPORTANCE OF LOCATION

A room corner is a perfect spot for the modern entertainment center. A television or video monitor can be viewed from a cozy cluster of seats that can fill the center of the viewing room. In contrast, a television placed in the center of a wall can be visually and functionally awkward since vacant spaces are created to either side of the primary viewing area. Anyone sitting

Barrie Graham's audiovisual center built alongside a fireplace is filled with clever shop-made features that coddle the equipment and make the unit versatile and easy to use. Photo by Barrie Graham.

Graham's Audiovisual Center

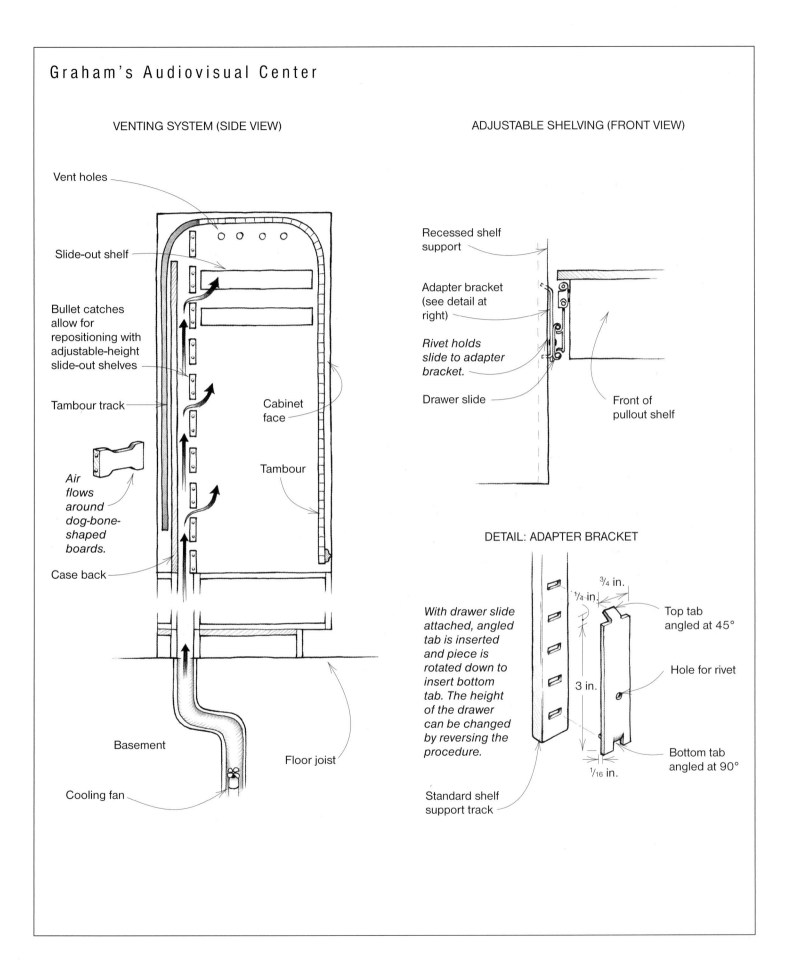

VENTING SYSTEM (SIDE VIEW)

Vent holes

Slide-out shelf

Bullet catches allow for repositioning with adjustable-height slide-out shelves

Tambour track

Air flows around dog-bone-shaped boards.

Case back

Cabinet face

Tambour

Basement

Floor joist

Cooling fan

ADJUSTABLE SHELVING (FRONT VIEW)

Recessed shelf support

Adapter bracket (see detail at right)

Rivet holds slide to adapter bracket.

Drawer slide

Front of pullout shelf

DETAIL: ADAPTER BRACKET

With drawer slide attached, angled tab is inserted and piece is rotated down to insert bottom tab. The height of the drawer can be changed by reversing the procedure.

Standard shelf support track

3/4 in.

1/4 in.

Top tab angled at 45°

Hole for rivet

3 in.

1/16 in.

Bottom tab angled at 90°

outside of the seating cluster may find the television hard to watch because of parallax, yet it is still a distraction, making it hard to use the space for other purposes. Corner-located speaker systems also tend to work extraordinarily well because converging walls often help create and funnel a rich, full sound out into the room. Also, with the furnishing angled across the corner, considerably more depth is available to accommodate large home-theater projection units.

The corner home-theater entertainment center designed by Dave Lehman and shown in the photo at left is an excellent example—it can be seen and heard well from nearly anywhere in the room. To achieve a tight fit where the sides of the unit touch the walls,

Dave Lehman's home theater extends across the corner of a room. The components on the left hide behind a smoked glass door (removed for the photo). Drawers on the right hold tapes, and the speakers sit behind removable grills alongside the small monitor. Photo by Steve Echols.

Though the entertainment center by Grady Mathews surrounds gable-end windows, its stepped-back upper cases and low window seat/drawer storage component allow ample natural light to penetrate the room. Photo by Grady Mathews.

Lehman, working for Swartzendruber Hardwood Creations of Goshen, Indiana, had the cabinetmakers extend the side walls slightly past the back of the case—allowing the sides to be scribed and cut precisely to the wall surface. The crown molding, decoratively grooved, was scribed to the out-of-level ceiling during installation. Black lacquer is the rich finish on this maple wood unit. To reduce the visual impact of deep scratches that might penetrate the lacquer top coat, Lehman had the light-colored maple stained black prior to being sprayed with the lacquer top coats.

Sometimes, the only available place to put the entertainment center is around a set of windows. In this case there may be some concern that the unit will diminish the penetration of natural light into the room. Cabinetmaker Grady Mathews, of Brier, Washington, solved this problem by stepping back the depth of the upper casework and by building a low drawer storage unit that can double as a window seat (see the bottom photo on the facing page). The drawers are divided by latticework to hold videotapes, CDs, and cassettes. The wood is cherry, with ebony handles.

ENTERTAINMENT CENTERS INCOGNITO

Many people dislike the look of modern electronic equipment and want their entertainment centers to look like furniture or perhaps even like an architectural form. Often, people want their audiovisual equipment to disappear entirely, with no visual clue whatsoever to its existence. Faced with this design challenge, cabinetmaker Michael Hoffer, of Espanola, New Mexico, created a credenza-like built-in furnishing (see the photo below) that manages to hide stereo components, a VCR, and a television set. Because his clients did not want even the speakers to show, he covered them with doors with a wood latticework. (Hoffer reports that his clients are unaware of a change in sound quality whether the doors are open or closed.)

Michael Hoffer's entertainment center in subtle Southwest styling completely hides the equipment behind decoratively pierced doors. Though the toe kick is taller than usual to accommodate the heating ductwork, it is visually reduced in height by the tasteful application of decorative trim. The wood louver duct covers are shop-made. Photo by Michael Hoffer.

Designer and cabinetmaker Tom Simmons, of Santa Barbara, California, wanted the entertainment center shown in the photos below to appear to be an architectural feature of the living room rather than a piece of furniture or built-in cabinet. When the circular case is rotated shut the unit has the look—to my eye at least—of a massive support column. Others see it as a form of pure sculpture—but I suspect few would guess this is a cabinet full of electronic gear.

Simmons based the construction of the unit around a commercially made semicircle of nine-ply veneer poplar plywood. After painting and installing shelving and cubbies to the curved plywood, he mounted the assembled unit to the surrounding case—sitting the base on a heavy-duty, ball-bearing TV turntable. A similar, but lighter, turntable provides the pivot point at the top.

Here's a different challenge: Create a traditional fireplace surround that

Built with commercially made plywood semicircles, this unit by Tom Simmons rotates open to change from a dramatic sculptural form to a functional entertainment center. Photos by Peter Malinowski.

secretly hides a television set and VCR. And here's a hint: Consider the large cavity that typically forms over a fireplace—why not put it to good use? This is exactly what Dale Patterson, of San Clemente, California, did when he decided to install the video equipment above the fireplace in his living room (see the photo at right). The trick, however, was to make the covering panel large enough to appear as the single panel that is traditionally found over a fireplace opening—yet somehow able to disappear into a pocket. Standard flipper pocket-door hardware could not accommodate the 40-in. width of the panel—at least 10 in. would remain sticking out of the wall pocket. Standard hardware also allows a panel no thicker than 1 in., which was a problem since the panel and the painting that hangs on it would together be more than 2 in. thick.

Patterson's solution was to mount the standard hardware to the inside of a box, which he in turn mounted on four center-mount-type slides (see the drawing at right). This setup gains additional movement for the panel, allowing the pocket to accommodate its full 40-in. width. To expose the television set, you swing the panel out to a 90° angle on its hidden piano hinge, then push it into the box. When the panel hits the back of the box, the box continues to recess into the wall as the sliding hardware takes over.

Dale Patterson's custom-made pocket-door panel over the fireplace disappears to reveal a television set and a VCR. Photo by Dale Patterson.

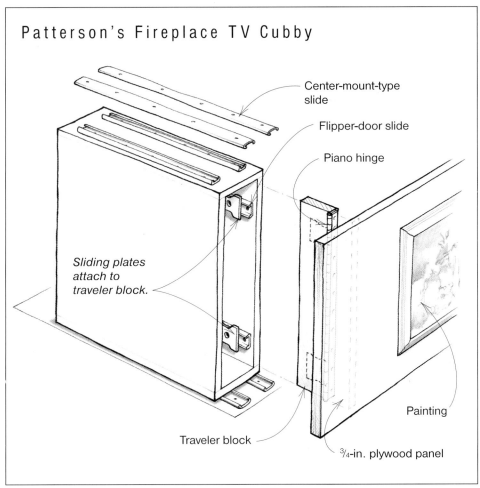

Patterson's Fireplace TV Cubby

Center-mount-type slide

Flipper-door slide

Piano hinge

Sliding plates attach to traveler block.

Traveler block

Painting

¾-in. plywood panel

Furnishings of solid African mahogany, designed by Albert Pastine, create a formal office/library in one corner of a living room. The large doors behind the desk hide computer equipment. Photo © Douglas A. Salin.

8
HOME OFFICES

Every home can benefit by having an office—because nearly all of us can make good use of a quiet, organized place in which to pay bills, write letters, or even run an out-of-home business (I wrote this book in an office built into the closed-in porch of my home). As you'll see in this chapter, the furnishings that create a home office can range from niches filled with elegant furniture-like built-ins to a tiny closet packed with efficient, space-saving casework to a sunken Japanese-style desk table.

Obviously, the designers of the home offices shown in the photos at left and on p. 132 had a bit more in mind than a quiet, unassuming place for writing checks. Instead, these elegantly styled and crafted built-in furnishings form an alcove within a home library to create an office that would make the CEO of any major corporation feel right at home (which was, perhaps, the actual intent of the design). Notice the similarity of layout: The desk is oriented so it faces into the room, imbuing the space with a sense of formality and its occupant with professional prestige—especially in the presence of visitors (and especially if the visitor's chair sits lower than that of the "CEO"!) In practical terms, an outward-facing orientation opens the niche to the surrounding space, making the office feel less dark and confining.

Albert Pastine, of San Francisco, California, in collaboration with interior designer Rhonda Luongo, designed an elegant office/library in solid African mahogany in one corner of a living room

Above: A formal office space, designed by Ned Forrest, was created by filling a semicircular alcove with a curved desk that terminates in two end cabinets. Below: cabinetmaker Dean Coley slides down the curved wall panel to conceal the computer. Photos by Sandor Nagyszalanczy.

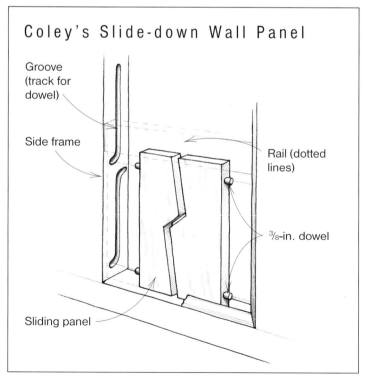

Coley's Slide-down Wall Panel

Groove (track for dowel)

Side frame

Rail (dotted lines)

⅜-in. dowel

Sliding panel

(see the photo on p. 132). The large doors behind the desk hide computer equipment. The faceted doors over display cubbies are veneered with bookmatched sepali. The furnishing was built by cabinetmaker Charley Marpet of Springfield, Oregon.

Cabinetmaker Dean Coley, of Watsonville, California, lined the semicircular alcove of a library with curved Honduras mahogany panels and cupboards to create an elegant office area directly behind an antique freestanding desk (see the photos on the facing page). To prevent computer hardware from ruining the traditional, formal ambience, the designer, Ned Forrest of Sonoma, California, asked Coley to make an inconspicuous door to conceal the monitor. (The keyboard mounts on a swing-out shelf that disappears under the counter when not in use.) Coley's solution was to leave one of the curved panels within the frame-and-panel wall loose, modifying it to slide up and down in a track (see the drawing on the facing page for construction details). To open the door, you press against its surface with a lifting motion—it easily slides up and then back, locking open. When closed, the "door" is indistinguishable from the rest of the wall paneling.

In addition to aesthetics, designers of home offices must also take ergonomics into account, particularly when planning computer workstations. For some guidelines on this subject and on proportioning office furniture in general, see the sidebar on p. 136.

The Office in a Room

Instead of making an office niche within a larger space, a designer might choose to fill an entire room with built-in office furnishings, fully defining the room's use in an attractive and efficient way. In the office shown in the photo at right,

counter surfaces and cupboards sweep around the perimeter of the room, creating spacious and versatile work areas. To a person seated in a wheeled office chair, any work station or storage space is just a quick kick away. Because the counters are continuous and of the same height, work stations can easily shift locations and accommodate more

than one person at a time. Ample natural lighting and a raised ceiling make the room appear more spacious than its limited floor area would suggest. The room was designed by Mark Simon and James C. Childress of Centerbrook Architects, Essex, Connecticut, and built by Doyle Construction of Vineyard Haven, Massachusetts.

This pentagonal room, designed by Centerbrook Architects, is completely ringed by cherry storage units, file drawers, counters, and writing tables. The raised ceiling and tall windows give the small room a feeling of spaciousness. Photo by Jeff Goldberg/Esto Photographics.

PROPORTIONING COMPUTER FURNITURE

Many of the dimensions and proportions of the office furnishings you design will be determined by office hardware (computers and related equipment) and file and document storage. An office for an artist or architect may also need specialized drawing surfaces and storage areas for plans (in rolls or as flats). And, of course, all work surfaces and casework must be proportioned to fit the people that will use them.

If it is possible and practical, measure the individual for whom the furnishings are to be built and adjust accordingly. Ideally, build a full-scale mockup (you can staple cardboard sheets to a wood frame) to ensure a perfect fit and a pleasing overall layout. Finally, choose an office chair with a stable base, a padded, adjustable back support, and a seat that is easily adjustable in height.

The drawing below, which has been adapted from *The Complete Guide to Building and Outfitting an Office in Your Home* (Betterway Books, 1994) gives ergonomically correct standard measurements for an office work station for an adult of average stature. Use them as a starting point for designing furnishings for the office. People who are taller or shorter may be more comfortable with an adjustment to these dimensions.

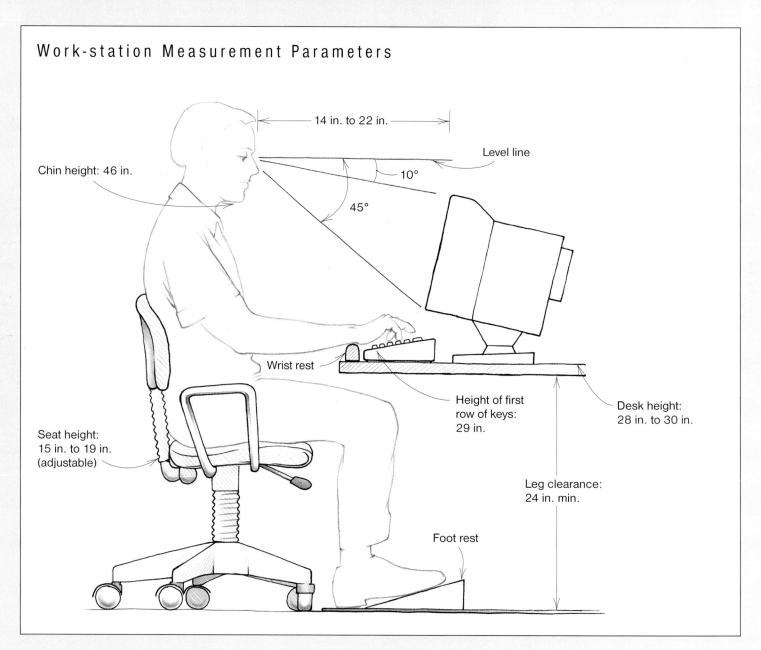

Work-station Measurement Parameters

14 in. to 22 in.

Level line

Chin height: 46 in.

10°

45°

Wrist rest

Height of first row of keys: 29 in.

Desk height: 28 in. to 30 in.

Seat height: 15 in. to 19 in. (adjustable)

Leg clearance: 24 in. min.

Foot rest

When sculptor Michael Braden, of Seattle, Washington, designed the office for his studio, he wanted more than good function and efficiency—he wanted the space to reflect and characterize his art. Braden worked with cabinetmaker Andrew de Klerk, also of Seattle, and the two created furnishings that seem to dance with a profusion of cubes, curves, and colors (see the photo at right). The copper covering on the writing counter —an unusual application for this material—makes a smooth writing surface and provides a splash of visual drama. The stepped drawers (whose faces are cut from the same board to ensure visual continuity) contain drawing supplies, while cubbies to the right store rolled blueprints.

To the right of the writing surface is a pencil drawer with a curved drawer face (see the photo at bottom right), which de Klerk created by laminating $\frac{1}{8}$-in.-thick ash strips against a form shaped to the curve.

Braden set the writing desk flat at a standard desk height and set the drawing surface slightly higher and at an angle. That way he can easily reach to the back of a large sheet of drawing paper.

A secret drawer slides out from under a file drawer (see the photo at near right). The plywood bottom panel of the secret drawer extends past its sides to form a tongue, which fits into a corresponding groove in the larger drawer to act as a drawer slide. The file drawer itself is mounted on heavy-duty, full-extension slides (to allow the drawer to pull all the way out of the case for easy access to the files at the back of the box.) Aniline-dyed wood surfaces contrast dramatically with the natural finish on the other surfaces.

The studio office of Seattle sculptor Michael Braden. A tasteful mix of materials and forms visually enlivens the small space while enhancing it functionally. Photo by Craig Wester.

A thin drawer under the much larger file drawer makes a good hiding place for sensitive documents. Photo by Jim Tolpin.

The curved face of the pencil drawer follows the line of the counter edge. Photo by Craig Wester.

This corridor-shaped space serves well as an architect's home office. Photo by Craig Wester.

Getting Creative with Small Spaces

Architect Ed Weinstein, of Seattle, Washington, made good use of a landing between a bedroom and a stairwell opening to create an at-home office for his architectural work (see the photo at left). Using bookshelves and cabinets to form the stairwell wall, he developed a corridor-like space—a very efficient configuration for the work patterns of an architect. In typical use, Weinstein quickly swivels 180° from the computer or drawing station to check reference books from the shelves or to draw supplies from the cabinets. Nothing is very far away. To store blueprints flat (which makes them much easier and faster to access) Weinstein had cabinet-maker Bill Walker, also of Seattle, build extra-wide drawers between the computer area and the drawing/writing desk area.

Notice how the large window, which runs nearly floor to ceiling, brings in abundant natural light to lend a feeling of spaciousness to what may have otherwise been an uncomfortably restrictive space. Track lighting illuminates both the books and the desk counter, while desk lamps provide task lighting. Also notice the careful attention to trim detail: The reveal around the shelf module on the far wall aligns precisely with the reveal on the window's head casing.

Even a closet can become a useful and attractive office with the help of some clever design and careful workmanship. Hiding his workspace behind a pair of bifold closet doors, designer/builder Christopher Beers, of Ramsey, New Jersey, elegantly constructed the built-in furnishings shown in the photo on the facing page in cherry wood and bird's-eye maple veneer. (The counter is surfaced with a marble-pattern laminate.) Though decidedly diminutive, this mini-office provides an ample writing surface, space for computer equipment including a printer, a pair of bookshelves, and a file cabinet (on the left side of the unit). The latter appears only on demand—it slides out into the knee well under the writing area on pocket-door hardware.

The pocket-door rollers are attached to wood mounting plates, which are in turn bolted to the top of the file cabinet. Slotted holes for the bolts provide side-to-side adjustment of rollers to ensure proper alignment to the track, and thus a smooth sliding action—see the drawing below). To bring out the file cabinet for access, Beers slides his chair back from the desk and grasps and pulls a handle mounted to the side of the case.

Here's an office built into a small brick-lined closet. (The bricks appeared when designer and builder Christopher Beers removed the drywall and studs to enlarge the space.) Though dark, the bricks give the space a rich, den-like feeling. Photo by Christopher Beers.

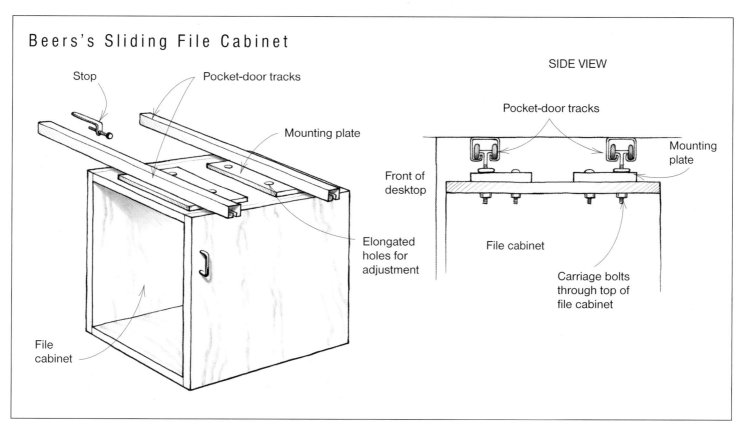

Beers's Sliding File Cabinet

Stop

Pocket-door tracks

Mounting plate

Elongated holes for adjustment

File cabinet

SIDE VIEW

Pocket-door tracks

Mounting plate

Front of desktop

File cabinet

Carriage bolts through top of file cabinet

The Office as Furnishing

You don't have to fill a room with furniture to create an office in a home—a furnishing can in itself do the job. It need only provide these basics: ample, well-lighted work surfaces; easy-to-access storage for office files, documents, and writing implements; computer hardware (if needed) at appropriate heights and orientations; some shelving for books. This furnishing may fill a wall from floor to ceiling, or it may stand on its own like a large piece of furniture.

Dean Coley, of Watsonville, California, designed and built some decidedly furniture-like cabinets and shelving in stained oak to create an office in one end of a den (see the photo below). Dropping the writing surface in the center of the unit (to the standard desk height of 29 in.) allows the side cabinets to extend high enough to contain a stack of two drawers for lateral hanging files and to accommodate a toe kick sized to match the room's

Dean Coley's floor-to-ceiling, wall-to-wall furnishing in stained oak creates an office in one end of a den. The unit features shop-made tambour doors and extensive lateral file drawers. Photo by George Hall.

baseboard. Reminiscent of a traditional rolltop desk, the tambour doors above the desk area hide the usual desktop clutter of cubbies crammed with pens and papers. Rather than using commercially made tambours, Coley made the doors in his shop so they would match the rest of the unit in coloration and grain (see the sidebar on pp. 142-143).

The office furnishings shown in the photos below and on p. 144 both back up a typical office desk, providing all the necessary storage and working surfaces. The desks are left uncluttered and available for writing and conferencing. The furnishing shown in the photo below, which was built by cabinetmaker Richard Wedler, of North Hollywood,

California, for a Hollywood producer, includes pull-out "sideboards" mounted on slide-out drawer hardware inserted into the ends of the unit's side walls. They hold shooting schedules for upcoming television shows. There are pull-out writing surfaces at either end of the counter, just above the bottom cupboards.

Richard Wedler's storage and desk system for a television producer forms its own side walls and ceiling. The counter surface is illuminated by light from recessed downlighting in the soffit. That is, by the way, a painting (not a window) over the desk. Photo by Richard Wedler.

Tambour doors look complex—even magical—in operation, but they are really quite straightforward. A tambour is nothing more than thin slats of wood held together at the back with a piece of glued-on canvas. You can buy ready-made tambours in a variety of sizes and species, but it is less limiting (and rather more fun) to make them yourself.

You start by making the slats (see the drawing below). Rip them on the table saw from either the face of the board to maintain a continuous, dramatic figure, or from the board's edge for a more subtle appearance. A chamfer or rounding of the face edges (easily done on a table-mounted router) is important both for aesthetics and for smooth operation when the tambour slides in its track. Cut the slats about 1 in. longer than necessary—you will trim the door square and to finished dimensions after applying the canvas.

To apply the canvas (see the bottom drawing on the facing page), lay the slats face down on a smooth, flat work surface. Use stops (any straight-edged wood scraps will do) to hold them tight against two boards placed at right angles to one another. Cut a piece of 6-oz. to 10-oz. weight canvas to size (make the width ¾ in. to 1 in. narrower than the finished width of the tambour) and coat one side with white or yellow glue (if you use yellow glue, you may want to thin it slightly with water to make it easier to spread). Also coat the back of the slats with glue and then lay on the canvas. Use a rubber roller or the rounded end of a piece of hardwood to smooth the glue flat and remove any bubbles. When the glue is dry, remove the side and top stops, lift out the assembled tambour, and cut it square and to final size.

To mount the tambour in a case, you can either choose a commercially made track or make one yourself by routing a

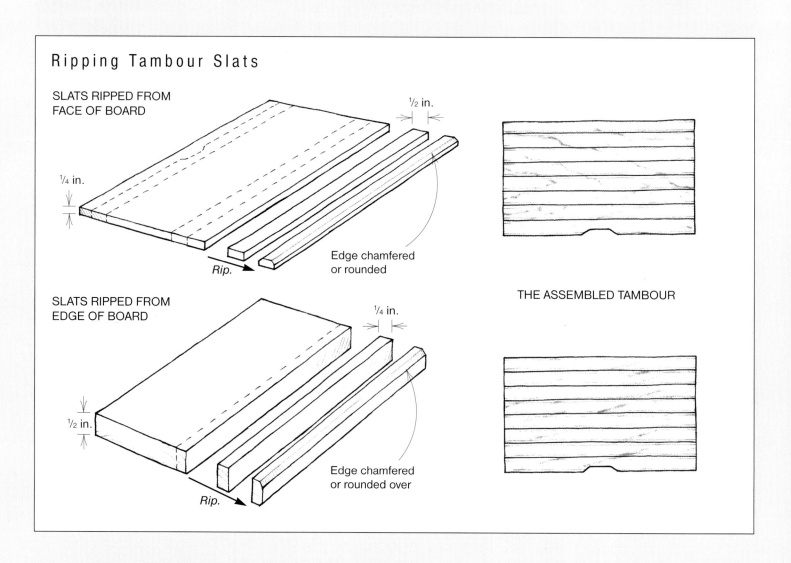

Ripping Tambour Slats

SLATS RIPPED FROM FACE OF BOARD

¼ in.

½ in.

Rip.

Edge chamfered or rounded

SLATS RIPPED FROM EDGE OF BOARD

½ in.

¼ in.

Rip.

Edge chamfered or rounded over

THE ASSEMBLED TAMBOUR

groove in a pair of boards (see the drawing at right). To ensure that the tambour will slide easily, without binding, use a template and a bearing-guided router bit to produce the curved tracking groove, which should be $\frac{1}{32}$ in. to $\frac{1}{16}$ in. bigger than the tambour profile. A bit of sanding and the occasional application of wax to the sliding surfaces should produce and maintain a smooth sliding action.

Routing a Groove for a Tambour Track

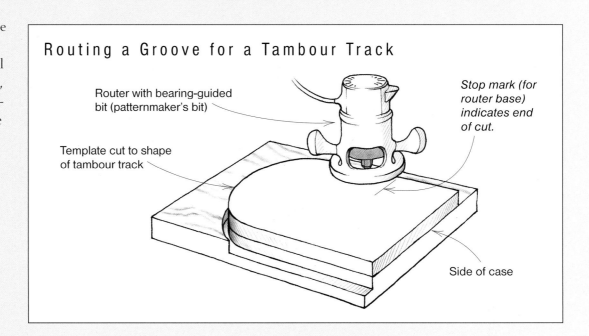

Router with bearing-guided bit (patternmaker's bit)

Stop mark (for router base) indicates end of cut.

Template cut to shape of tambour track

Side of case

Applying the Canvas

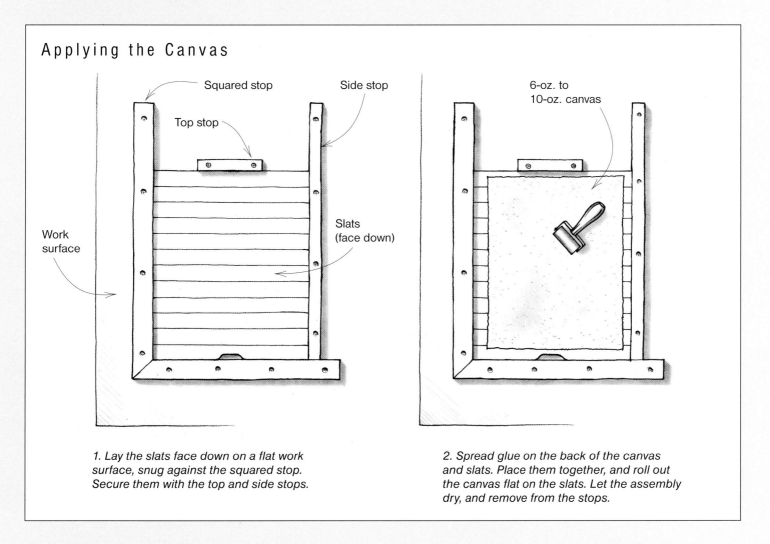

Squared stop

Side stop

Top stop

6-oz. to 10-oz. canvas

Work surface

Slats (face down)

1. Lay the slats face down on a flat work surface, snug against the squared stop. Secure them with the top and side stops.

2. Spread glue on the back of the canvas and slats. Place them together, and roll out the canvas flat on the slats. Let the assembly dry, and remove from the stops.

Tom Simmons's unit (see the photos at left and below) encloses so much computer equipment that he calls the furnishing a "cyber-secretary." With the doors closed, the unit reveals only an attractive selection of books and knickknacks on its glass shelving (which is tastefully highlighted by low-voltage downlighting). The vertical doors in the center bay ride on flipper-door hardware—the hinged pilaster moldings hide the door edges when flipped and slid into their open position. The cubbies in the side bays open as

Clean in line and form when closed, the "cyber-secretary" by Tom Simmons holds a great deal of electronic equipment, including a geosynchronous clock. When open, the flipper doors hide behind the hinged pilaster columns. Photos by Peter Malinowski.

The design of Len Brackett's unusual study desk was influenced by the traditional Japanese *kotatsu*, a low covered table. The surrounding floor of tatami mats provides plenty of additional room to spread out paperwork. Photo by James Kline.

horizontal flip doors. As in Wedler's unit (see p. 141), pull-out writing surfaces augment the facing desk—although here they hide behind false drawer fronts.

Office furnishings don't have to be high tech. Consider, for example, the desk shown in the photo above. Influenced by *kotatsu,* the low covered tables typical of traditional Japanese homes, Len Brackett, of Nevada City, California, created this study and writing desk in an alcove of his own home. The design is simple, unobtrusive, and beautiful. A recess into the floor (see the drawing at right) provides leg room. Natural light, filtered softly through a latticework of small branches, plays across the writing surface, while a sliding translucent shutter of frosted glass can eliminate glare as needed.

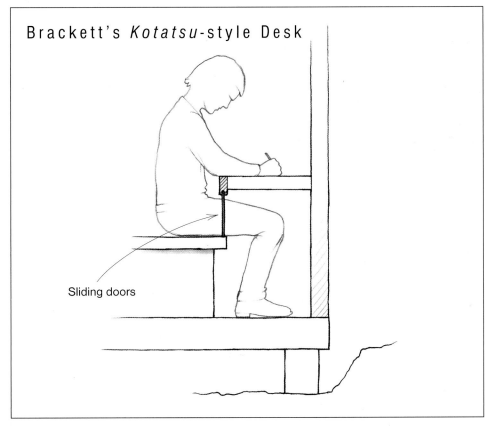

Brackett's *Kotatsu*-style Desk

Sliding doors

9
FAMILY ROOMS

The family room is a place where the members of a family can come together to relax, to play, to create, to entertain, or to be entertained. In this room, the built-in furnishing systems are often more extensive and inclusive than library wall systems or audiovisual centers—besides providing for books and entertainment systems, family-room furnishings may also be asked to contain arts and crafts supplies and work areas, musical instruments, play spaces for children, seating (including window seating), and hide-away beds. Many family rooms also include the adult "rec room"—the wet bar.

Though the family room is generally an informal space, it doesn't have to be. Architect Albert Pastine, of San Francisco, California, certainly didn't think informal when he created a dramatic space within a large California-modern home (see the photo on the facing page). Instead, he imbued the room with crisp, cleanly finished

This formal, arched-ceiling family room resounds with the colors and textures of solid-color lacquered cabinets accompanied by dramatic fabrics and art pieces. Designed by Albert Pastine in collaboration with interior designer Rhonda Luongo. Photo © Douglas A. Salin.

built-in cabinetry and trim, creating display places for fine artwork and play places for family activities. Pull-out foot rests (or seats for children) are stored below the integrated window seat, while the cabinets to one side of the fireplace camouflage pull-out carts for audiovisual equipment. Notice how the cap defining the top of the seating extends to form an arch over the fireplace, unifying the mantel surround with the built-in furnishings. The work was built by Charley Marpet (Marpet Fine Woodworking) of Springfield, Oregon.

Keith and Margaret Kervin, of North Bay, Ontario, took a completely different tack. In response to a houseful of creative and active children, they designed and built a furnishing to store the burgeoning collection of games and art supplies and to provide an ample, though well-contained, activity area (see the photo below). The design—clean and free of superfluous elements—was motivated primarily by economy and function. To keep costs down and construction straightforward, the builder, Michael Kervin (MGK Construction and Design), also of North Bay, framed the alcove and its partitions with $2\frac{1}{2}$-in. steel studs and sheathed with $\frac{1}{2}$-in. drywall. The desktop was made by gluing and screwing together two layers of $\frac{5}{8}$-in. particleboard and then applying laminate to the top, bottom, and front edge. (Laminate on the bottom surface controls moisture exchange with the air, and thus the potential for warpage.) The doors and shelving are $\frac{5}{8}$-in. melamine, and the base molding is painted medium-density fiberboard (MDF). Carpeting covers the rest of the playroom floor, but the Kervins wisely chose easy-to-clean and durable linoleum for the area in and around the game and art center.

When the growing family of Richard and Emily Westrick, of Dallastown, Pennsylvania, needed a bit more room, the space over their attached garage beckoned. With a lot of planning (not to mention hands-on work), they turned it into a multipurpose room for arts and crafts, reading, writing letters, playing, and putting up guests—all without sacrificing the dead storage an attic typically provides. The top photo on the facing page show the results.

After gutting the space, the Westricks raised up one side of the roof (literally—but that's another story), refinished the floor and roof, and then created an extensive system of redwood-faced built-in furnishings throughout the space (see the drawing on the facing page). Book and game shelves flank a sewing-center cabinet complete with a hide-away, fold-down sewing table, which is accessed by pivoting aside a bank of storage shelves. Along the full length of the opposite wall, massive pull-out storage bins contain a family's worth of dead storage.

In the northwest corner of the room (see the bottom photo on the facing page), a clothing storage closet hides behind a motor-driven vertical-slat tambour door, which is activated by a recycled food-mixer motor. Since the closet didn't require full floor-to-ceiling height, the Westricks installed a false floor, creating room underneath for a roll-out bed. A guide track ensures against jams and provides a smooth rolling action. The room has two entrances—a door and a rolling barrel (guess which one the kids use?). The space above the barrel forms an open loft—a club house and retreat for the little people.

When cabinetmaker Marv Schupp, of London, Ontario, was approached by clients who wanted a massive storage furnishing for a new family room, they knew exactly what they didn't want:

In Keith and Margaret Kervin's informal family room, straightforward cabinetry forms a warm, well-lighted storage and activity center. Photo by Keith Kervin.

In an extensive attic remodel, Richard and Emily Westrick created a multipurpose room filled with clever and functional built-ins. This view toward one corner shows a desk, bookshelves, a sewing center, and a craft cabinet. Photo by Bob Brode.

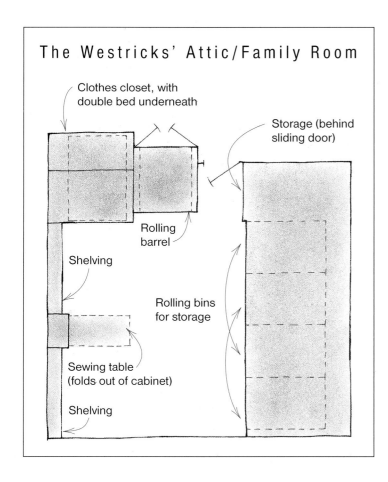

The Westricks' Attic/Family Room

Clothes closet, with double bed underneath

Storage (behind sliding door)

Rolling barrel

Shelving

Rolling bins for storage

Sewing table (folds out of cabinet)

Shelving

At one end of the Westricks' family room is a unique rolling-barrel entrance for children, with a play loft above. To its left, a roll-out bed slides under a clothes closet concealed behind a motorized tambour door. Photo by Bob Brode.

a big piece of furniture. Instead, they wanted a unit that would appear to be a part of the structure of the room and not an add-on. Luckily, they found the right man, for Schupp specializes in creating built-ins that look not only as if they belong there, but also as if they have always been there. According to Schupp, the key to success lay in educated proportion and styling and careful workmanship throughout construction and installation.

Schupp began the creation of this storage unit with a scale model in cardboard to check its proportions. (Unlike a drawing, a model can be viewed from any angle so the eye can compare one surface against another.)

Changing the model as necessary, Schupp worked with the design until it had pleasing dimensions that were harmonious from any predicted vantage point within the family room. To make the unit appear structurally significant, Schupp decided to add width and recessed panels to the center stiles to make them appear to the eye as support columns with mass and function—an architectural element of the room (see the photo below). The speakers to either side of the unit are not boxed in, so the owners can replace them in the future with other-sized units.

Next, Schupp drew a full-scale rendering of the piece. This allowed him to create concise cutting templates for

many of the components—especially the top frieze boards that would meet the varying angles of the cathedral ceiling. He also used the rendering as a graphic database for the master cut lists that would direct the cutting of the ¾-in. veneer-core birch plywood and solid poplar into the components of the modules. Schupp assembled the modules on site, visually tying them to the ceiling and wall surfaces with carefully installed moldings.

Though the furnishings shown in the photo on the facing page are nowhere near the scale of Schupp's wall unit, they shared a similar design goal: to appear to be a part of the original design and construction of the home—to look

This family-room storage and shelf unit by Marv Schupp is 11 ft. wide and runs from the floor to the 10-ft.-high gabled ceiling. The consciously architectural design makes the unit appear structurally significant to the space. Photo by Michael Jordan.

Marble-topped cubbies lining the walls of a music room provide storage for sheet music and tasteful and effective camouflage for steam radiators as well. Photo by Jim Price.

architectural and not like furniture. In this family room graced with a grand piano, the client asked cabinetmaker Jim Price, of Newport, Kentucky, for shelving that could hold music books and sheet music and provide a surface for potted plants. The client also hoped that the furnishing would hide the ugly steam radiators that marched blatantly around the perimeter of the room—somehow they had to be deleted from the visual landscape of the room.

Price responded to the challenge by designing a straightforward set of cubbies in painted poplar and lauan mahogany. The top of the unit—a framework supporting an inlay of white marble—runs even with the window sills and appears continuous with them. A wood framework surrounding painted 26-ga. perforated sheet metal hides the radiators (see the drawing at right). Inside the unit, a rolled piece of sheet metal directs the heat away from the overlying shelf and out through the metal facing. A removable side panel covers the radiator controls.

Price's Cover for a Steam Radiator

CROSS SECTION

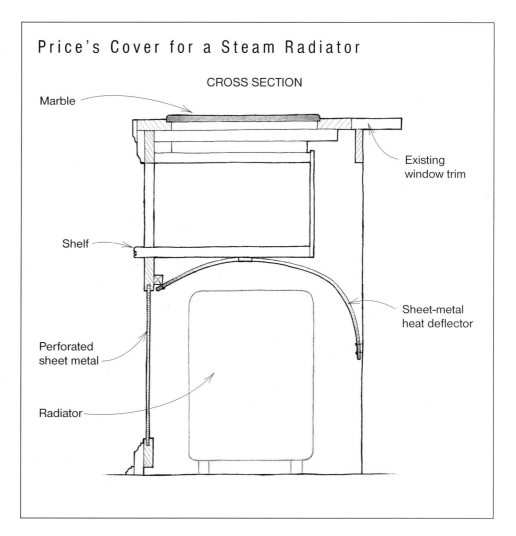

Marble

Existing window trim

Shelf

Sheet-metal heat deflector

Perforated sheet metal

Radiator

Built entirely from solid wood, this family-room hutch by Steve Winchester is assured of a long life through structural features that can compensate for the inevitable movement of the wood. Photo by Steve Winchester.

Because the owner wanted the units to be removable, Price realized that the original interior trim should not be disturbed in any way—that way, there would be no need to make up replacement moldings if the cubbies were removed. Of course, the clients also wanted the unit to look as if it had always been there. These contradictory demands made installation a bit tricky: Price began by prefinishing the unit so all the priming and painting would be completed prior to installation. Then, temporarily sitting the unit in place on the carpet (to which he had first applied wide masking tape), Price traced its

outline. He then removed the unit and cut the carpet to the line.

To level the unit quickly and precisely to the window sills, Price added shop-made leveling feet to the floor board. When the leveled unit was set back in place, he scribed and cut the top frame to fit against the sills and the side panels to fit around the baseboard.

Taking advantage of a closet along one wall of a family room-to be, cabinet-maker Steve Winchester, of Gilmanton, New Hampshire, filled the space with a storage and display hutch made entirely from solid ash—a choice that honored the tradition and quality of the

woodworking in the rest of the house. Stained, the ash closely matches the original—and no longer obtainable—chestnut (see the photo above).

To hide the effects of wood movement that might occur with the use of solid wood, Winchester employed a variety of techniques: tongue-and-groove side boards and back boards that can move independently of one another, mortised frame connections that hide the evidence of dimensional change, floating-panel doors that can move without changing the overall size of the door itself, and fastenings that allow the components of the unit to expand or contract without splitting or buckling. In addition, moldings cover the joint lines to camouflage gaps. For illustrations and more detailed information about these techniques, see the sidebar on pp. 154-155.

Window Seats

"Our love for window places is not a luxury but an organic intuition," says Christopher Alexander in *A Pattern Language,* his breakthrough book on architectural design. It's true, people are naturally drawn to windows—if we have a choice of where to stand or sit, we nearly always gravitate toward a spot bathed in natural light. Alexander felt so strongly that seating should take advantage of "window places" that he came to believe that "...without a window seat a room may keep you in a state of perpetual unresolved conflict and tension." I would add that a window seat not only soothes the human spirit, but can also do great things for the interior architecture of a home. It is a place where rich textures, vibrant colors, and stimulating geometric patterns can come together to create a provocative, yet comfortable, space within a larger room.

The strong vertical lines of the diminutive window shown in the photo at right respond to the tall, thin trees in view outside, while the tall, narrow shape of the alcove lends visual drama to the gabled ceiling inside house. Facing south, this window seat, designed by Jim Sterling, of Portland, Maine, and built by Sewall Associates, also of Portland, is bathed in light (if not sunshine) throughout most of the day.

Elegant in its simple geometry, this tiny window seat by Jim Sterling beckons you to partake of its pleasures. Photo © Brian Vanden Brink.

The casework in this chapter—and throughout much of the rest of this book—is built mainly from man-made sheet stock. Only face frames, moldings, door frames, and occasional recessed panels are of solid wood. And for good reason: Sheet goods are predictably stable—they do not change significantly in dimension or flatness with seasonal fluctuations of humidity inside a typical home.

Solid woods, however, are not inert. Many species can move as much as 1/8 in. per foot of width with a 20% change in humidity. Indeed, any board will shrink to some degree in width and thickness as it dries, and will similarly swell in response to humidity. (However, the change in length of a board is insignificant.)

So why use solid wood at all? Because woodworkers—and people who enjoy the fruits of their labors—appreciate the durability, beauty, and integrity of solid wood. Fortunately, there are various construction strategies that can help a solid-wood structure cope with seasonal fluctuations in humidity without self-destructing.

SPLINE-JOINING BOARDS TO WIDTH

Narrow boards can be joined together with edge splines to form wide panels (see the top drawing at right). A chamfer, bead, or kerf along the edge creates a shadow line that hides seasonal shrinkage gaps. The groove for the spline can be made with a slotting cutter on a shaper or table-mounted router, or with a dado-blade setup on the table saw. The spline is made from strips of plywood or cut from a board. In the latter case, the spline must be cut across the grain so it won't change in length or be subject to splitting. Splines are not glued in place. Instead, they float so each board can move independent of the others, preventing splitting if the boards shrink in width.

FASTENING COUNTER SURFACES

To secure a wide solid-wood surface such as a countertop, only its front edge is fixed (to maintain its alignment with the underlying molding or face frame). The rest of the surface is fastened with movable cleats or hardware fasteners (see the bottom drawing at right), run in a groove, or captured between side panels. A gap at the back of the counter allows for expansion—otherwise swelling boards could hit the back wall and push out the front of the case.

When individual tongue-and-groove boards are fastened, one fastener (either a glued biscuit or a metal fastener such as a screw or nail) is located at the center of each board. This strategy allows each board to change dimension around its own centerline, minimizing the effect of that change on the surrounding boards.

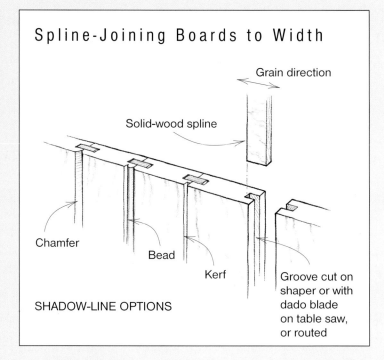

Spline-Joining Boards to Width

Grain direction

Solid-wood spline

Chamfer

Bead

Kerf

Groove cut on shaper or with dado blade on table saw, or routed

SHADOW-LINE OPTIONS

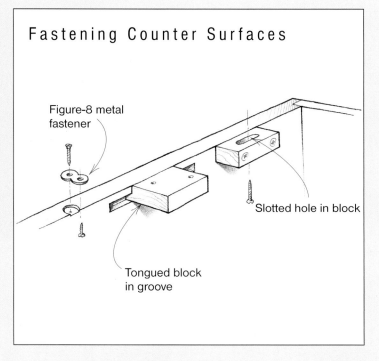

Fastening Counter Surfaces

Figure-8 metal fastener

Slotted hole in block

Tongued block in groove

HIDING JOINT LINES

Whenever possible, it's a good idea to try to hide the junction of two boards where swelling or shrinkage would create a noticeable gap. As shown in the drawing below, moldings can be applied to cover joints or to create shadow lines that distract the eye from the gap in a joint line.

Where a stile meets a head casing, a gap is likely to appear if the head casing shrinks in width. In the detail drawing below left, a shallow mortise in the head casing captures the top of the stile. Should the header shrink, no gap will appear. The mortise also helps keep the face of the stile flat.

FLOATING FRAME AND PANEL

Frame-and-panel construction is an ancient, and successful, design solution that allows cabinetmakers to build wide doors without fear of warping or splitting—an all-too-common malady of wide plank doors. The secret lies in a floating panel set into a surrounding framework: The panel can shrink and swell within the frame without changing the overall dimensions or shape of the door itself.

To make a floating-panel door, the panel is cut to size so there will be a gap of $\frac{1}{8}$ in. between its perimeter and the bottom of the receiving groove in the surrounding frame. During assembly, glue in the frame corners must not touch (and cement) the corner of the panel. One trick is to coat the panel corners with candle wax. To keep the floating panel centered in its frame, a hole is drilled through the frame and and a pin is installed into the panel. Alternatively, strips of foam weatherstripping may be inserted into the surrounding groove, as shown in the drawing below right.

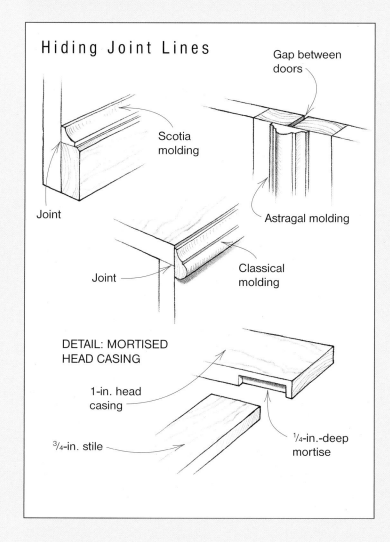

Hiding Joint Lines

Gap between doors

Scotia molding

Joint

Astragal molding

Joint

Classical molding

DETAIL: MORTISED HEAD CASING

1-in. head casing

$\frac{3}{4}$-in. stile

$\frac{1}{4}$-in.-deep mortise

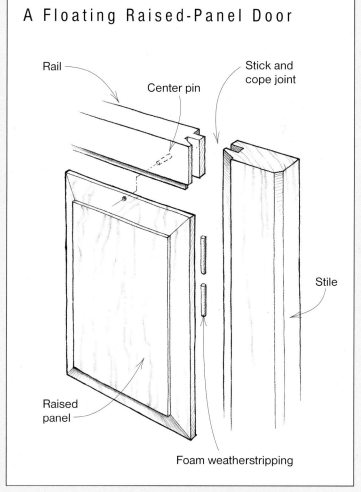

A Floating Raised-Panel Door

Rail

Center pin

Stick and cope joint

Stile

Raised panel

Foam weatherstripping

This built-in couch and end tables by South Mountain Co. were made from cypress salvaged from defunct beer vats. Decorative cutouts in the couch's apron also serve as vents for heating ducts. Photo by Derrill Bazzy.

In contrast, the space made available by the large window bay of a family room inspired the designers of South Mountain Co., of Chilmark, Massachusetts, to fill it with more than a simple bench. To make the most comfortable space possible, they built in a full-size, custom-made upholstered sofa that, together with end tables, fills the entire window alcove (see the photo above). By day, you can sit crosswise and enjoy the lake-front view; by night, you lean back to face the flickering fireplace directly opposite the alcove.

The window seat shown in the photo on the facing page and designed by its owner, Carol Hasse, of Port Townsend, Washington, is one of a pair flanking a set of French doors centered on a window wall spanning the length of the family room. By day, the seats are warm and sunny spots for reading and napping. At night, they can convert to beds. Cabinetmaker Alex Spear, also of Port Townsend, built the seats from local clear vertical-grain old-growth fir.

Carol Hasse's window seat/daybed projects the family room into the conifer forest that surrounds her Pacific Northwest home. Photo by Craig Wester.

Tom Bosworth's window seat converts to a full-length guest bed (see the drawing below). Photo by Craig Wester.

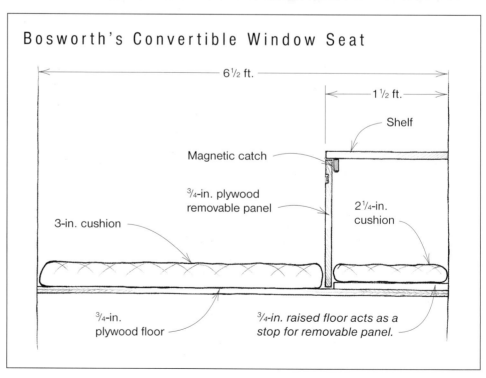

Bosworth's Convertible Window Seat

6½ ft.

1½ ft.

Shelf

Magnetic catch

¾-in. plywood removable panel

3-in. cushion

2¼-in. cushion

¾-in. plywood floor

¾-in. raised floor acts as a stop for removable panel.

The bench-style seat in the photo on the facing page sits before a large window and between built-in book shelving to create a much-appreciated and well-used space within architect Tom Bosworth's own island retreat. To add to the versatility, the sitting bench, which was built by Peter Kilpatrick, of Friday Harbor, Washington, converts to a full-length bed when the panel under the bottom shelf, which is held in place with a magnetic catch, is removed (see the drawing on the facing page). Two large drawers mounted on heavy-duty, full-extension side-mount drawer slides keep bedding close by and ready for use. A built-in wall lamp creates a cozy reading alcove at night.

Also designed by Tom Bosworth, the two window seat/daybeds shown in the photo below flank a raised hearth in a client's master bedroom. Under the seats, large drawers, mounted on heavy-duty extension slides, provide handy storage for bedding. Firewood is kept in two plywood drawers under the hearth. Galvanized steel sheets lining the interior of the drawers prevent any bugs or moisture in the firewood from escaping into the house. The unit was built by Dan Paulson of Friday Harbor, Washington.

Built-in drawers under a hearth are handy for storing firewood, while flanking daybeds offer comfortable sleeping or reading spaces. Designed by Tom Bosworth. Photo by Craig Wester.

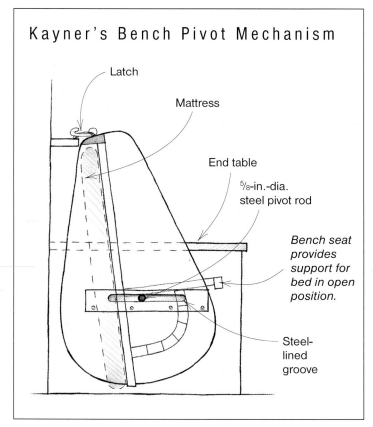

Kayner's Bench Pivot Mechanism

Latch

Mattress

End table

$5/8$-in.-dia.
steel pivot rod

*Bench seat
provides
support for
bed in open
position.*

Steel-
lined
groove

With a pull-down motion, Alex Kayner's built-in bench (above) converts to a futon bed for overnight guests (right). The drawing above right shows how the pivot mechanism works. Photos © Brian Vanden Brink.

House and boat builder Alex Kayner, of Bar Harbor, Maine, built the bench seat shown in the photo at left on the facing page of local white birch, finishing it to a high sheen with multiple coats of varnish. The simplicity and elegance of Kayner's design make it difficult to perceive that this bench can transform in seconds to a full-size futon bed (see the photo at right on the facing page). But it does—all you have to do is unhook two brass latches and rotate the back of the bench forward and down, and then slide it forward several inches. The bench pivots on a beefy (⁵⁄₈ in. O.D.), full-length hidden steel rod protruding into steel-lined grooves mortised into the sides of the built-in tables at either end (see the drawing on the facing page for details). Kayner worked out the mechanism on a plywood mockup to be sure that it would operate correctly and smoothly.

Wet Bars

Not all family rooms have a wet bar, but some wouldn't be complete without one. Wet bars range from long sit-down counters amid cabinetry festooned with complex moldings and carvings to a simple sink counter and cupboard combination tucked into a niche or closet. One wet bar featured here found its place on a stairway corner landing— a tricky location for tipplers! Another (see the photo at right) serves a large family and guest entertainment room through an interior window. All wet bars, though, do two things: They have a sink for washing glassware, and they provide storage for beverages, glasses, and attendant paraphernalia.

What happens when your clients purchase a 400-year-old manor in the English countryside, transport it piece

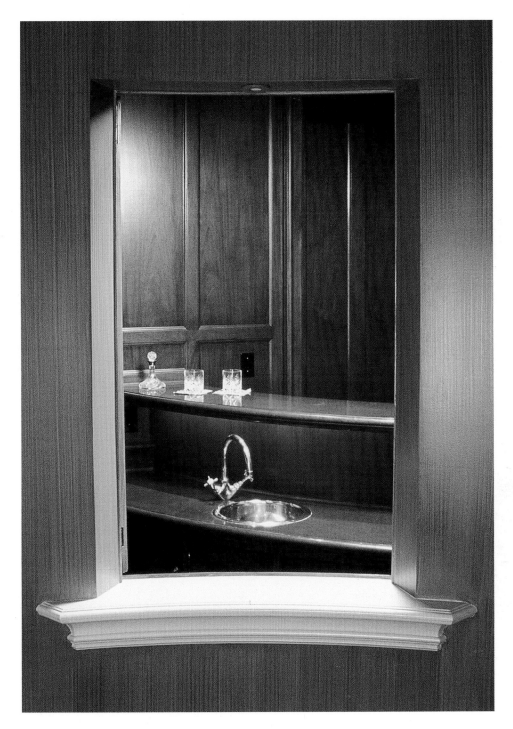

This wet bar, rich in solid Honduras mahogany paneling and counters, hides in a room to one side of a large family room. Designed by Ned Forrest of Sonoma, Calif., and built by Dean Coley of Watsonville, Calif. Photo by Sandor Nagyszalanczy.

Welcome to The Lion's Den! This authentic period-style bar was built into one wing of an English manor house transported from England to Canada. Designed and built by Dean Jackson (Custom Wood Designs); carvings by Siggi Buhler. Photo by Pam Carnell.

by piece to Canada, where it is painstakingly reassembled, and then ask you to build a bar into one of the semicircular wings? If you are Dean Jackson of Toronto, Canada, you build something like this: a marble-topped bar supported by hand-carved lion heads backed by a curved run of oak cupboards featuring lead-glazed, cut-glass windows and authentic period moldings—including a curved cornice (see the photo on the facing page).

The curved components posed a barroom-full of special challenges: To curve the oak raised panels of the doors, Jackson moistened one side of the panel while applying heat to the other, and pressed it into a form. When the panel achieved the curve, he attached the top and bottom rails (which had previously been laminated to the curve) and proceeded to glue up the frame. To make a ventilation grill for the built-in refrigerator in the cabinet under the bar counter, Jackson cut a series of slots in the face of an oak board and then steamed and clamped it to a curved form (see the photo at right). (Jackson plunge-cut the slots on the table saw using stops attached to the rip fence to control the length of the cut—a table-mounted router is another—and perhaps safer—option.)

To make the curved crown molding, Jackson first laminated the cove portion in position, using thin strips of wood with the edges precut to a sequence of angles. He installed the strips by gluing and nailing them in place (see the drawing above right). Each successive layer hid the nails of the last. When the glue dried, Jackson formed the curve with the front roller of a belt sander, then smoothed it with a curved cabinet scraper. Finally, he nailed steam-bent moldings to the top and bottom of the completed cove to finish off the profile.

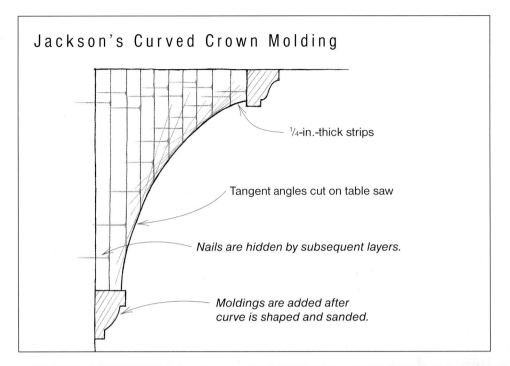

Jackson's Curved Crown Molding

¼-in.-thick strips

Tangent angles cut on table saw

Nails are hidden by subsequent layers.

Moldings are added after curve is shaped and sanded.

A solid oak board, pierced with slots and steam bent to the curve, provides ventilation for a built-in refrigerator. Photo by Dean Jackson.

A cherry wet-bar counter and painted cabinets by Joseph Arentz and Jim Tshudy slip behind a sliding barn-type door—out of sight and out of mind when not in use. Vertical liquor drawers beneath the sink and thin drawers that hang under the upper cabinets maximize the limited space. Photos by Joseph Arentz.

The wet bar shown in the photos on the facing page not only avoids protruding into the family room, but also disappears entirely behind a sliding barn-type door—an admirable quality for a bar when the preacher (or a teetotaling relative) comes to visit. The inspiration for this arrangement came as Joseph Arentz and Jim Tshudy, of Stephens, Pennsylvania, worked to remodel a 200-year-old Pennsylvania log cabin. When a new sunroom addition joined the existing structure, an odd-shaped space appeared. Applying a bit of clever design work, the two were able to fill the space with a solid cherry-wood countertop, cupboards (coated in traditional red milk paint), a sink, and a built-in refrigerator.

To maximize the narrow space, Tshudy built tall and thin vertical drawers that could each store up to two dozen liquor bottles. When the drawers are slid out on their full-extension drawer slides, the bottles are easy to see and easy to reach. The thin drawers fitted under the hanging cabinets (and just below eye level when extended) contain dish towels, napkins, small knives, mixing spoons, and coasters.

In another example of making the most of an unusual space, Bill Capps and Dave Knapp, of Somerset, Pennsylvania, designed and constructed a wet bar and liquor storage cabinetry on a stair landing (see the photo at right). It's a reasonable location (unless you are tipsy) since it falls between a living room and family room, each of which is used for entertaining. Capps built the bar from cedar to match the rest of the home's interior. At his client's suggestion, he faced the bar counter with wine bottles (empty, of course) for an unusual decorative effect. Ticket stubs from sports events under the bar counter's glass surface lend additional visual—and conversational—interest. To bring light down to the server's station (and to illuminate an interesting collection of bottles), Capps allowed the top shelf to run across the room corner, creating a soffit with an ample overhang in which to install spot lighting.

This wet bar by Bill Capps and Dave Knapp sits on a stair landing between a living room and a family room. Photo by Bill Capps.

10
UTILITY ROOMS

In the utility rooms of the modern home, built-ins are a pervasive presence. Sink vanities, tub enclosures, and other storage systems make bathrooms efficient and attractive spaces to be in. Built-in cabinets form laundry work centers, often allowing the room to be used for multiple purposes. In closets and dressing rooms, clever furnishings (including elevators) maximize the limited space.

The dressing room shown in the photo on the facing page is composed entirely of built-ins. Designed by Mark Simon, of Centerbrook Architects and Planners, Essex, Connecticut, and built by Ricketson Woodwork, of Hartford, Connecticut, it features louvered-door closets and a custom-made bureau built into an alcove.

Of all the areas in a home, utility rooms are places where stand-alone furniture is simply not up to the task—and where cabinet-makers may find their greatest challenges.

Built-in closets and a bureau designed by Mark Simons lend elegance and function to a dressing room. Photo by Jeff Goldberg/ Esto Photographics.

In most modern bathrooms, the vanity is essential: This furnishing provides storage space for toiletries, cleansers, paper goods, and makeup supplies, while at the same time supporting a counter that contains the sink. The traditional vanity, as exemplified in the photo on the facing page, however, is sinkless—it's just a sitdown table with a mirror.

The built-in vanities that are shown on the following pages are gleaned from new homes and remodels currently being built around the country.

Phillipus Sollman, of Bellefonte, Pennsylvania, built this furniture-quality vanity in solid cherry facing a biscuit-joined ¾-in. plywood interior. The attention to detail is remarkable: Texture changes on the backsplash match similarly textured door panels, and the subtle arch under the mirror and the gently swelling face of the vanity match the contours of the sink. The wide drawers flanking the doors are for linens (there is no closet) and slide out on wood runners. Photo by Phillipus Sollman.

This traditional-style vanity provides a comfortable, well-appointed, and well-lit makeup area. Though the solid Honduras mahogany unit approaches furniture in style and execution, it sits permanently in place on a tile-faced toe-kick frame. Builder Del Cover of San Diego, California, developed the design to match the style of the existing mirror—note how the edging of the counter echoes the profile of the mirror frame. Photo by Del Cover.

To maximize the space within a narrow bathroom and to avoid obstructing the doorway, designer and builder Jim Bringham, of Antelope, California, held the depth of the vanity to 12⅜ in.—except in the area of the sink. Here, the upper portion of the unit swells out into a curve that contains the round porcelain sink. To form the curved apron, Bringham cut a series of ⅛-in.-wide saw kerfs across the back of a strip of ¾-in. maple plywood and then clamped the now flexible strip over two curved horizontal plywood partitions. Notice that the apron piece runs the full length of the vanity face tomaintain a continuous grain pattern with the two flanking drawer faces. Photo by Jim Bringham.

This unit, designed and built by Alex Spear, of Port Townsend, Washington, strives to minimize its footprint within the bathroom. The pine wood counter—supported on a Honduras mahogany case—holds the sink and provides shelf space to either side. Curved open shelves attached to the cabinet side walls help tie the case visually to the sweep of the counter surface. The owners chose fabric rather than doors to cover the plumbing to ensure ventilation and to allow an occasional change in color scheme. The glossy finish—a marine spar varnish applied by yacht finisher Julie Maynard— provides ample protection and a rich color. Photo by Craig Wester.

The bathroom of an Adirondack Mountain style home is furnished with this slate-topped red-cedar vanity. The twig door pulls, towel pegs and light-shade supports, and the mirror surrounded with birch-bark trim, further contribute to the ambience of a rustic lodge. Designed by architect Peter Bohlin, of Pittsburgh, Pennsylvania, and built by Andreassen and Nicholson Construction, of Hague, N. Y. Photo © Brian Vanden Brink.

A built-in, all-maple continuous vanity unit encloses a sink and a raised tub. Wainscot carries across the drawer and door faces to wrap around the tub area, and the overall shape of the unit is reflected by the massive curved soffit above. Note the unusually high toe kick: it allows the step leading up to the tub to be set at a useful height while at the same time letting it blend in with the kick. Multiple layers of protective clear finish and ample room ventilation protect the extensive wood surfaces. Designed by Mark Simon, of Centerbrook Architects and Planners, Essex, Connecticut, and built by Ricketson Woodwork, of Hartford, Connecticut. Photo by Jeff Goldberg/Esto Photographics.

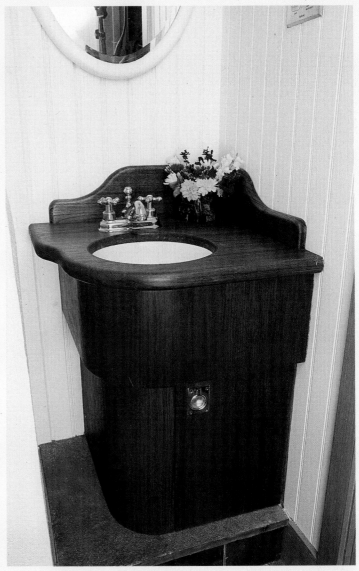

This white oak and walnut vanity, built for a desert home in southern California, shows how a unifying design element—here, the tilework—can visually tie a built-in unit to the rest of the space. The ventilation grill was made by inserting short lengths of wood into angled dadoes cut into two horizontal trim strips. Designed by Jim Tolpin, of Port Townsend, Washington, and built by Tolpin and Chris Marrs, also of Port Townsend. Photo by Jim Tolpin.

A tiny bathroom with a tiny sink calls for a tiny vanity. That's how this all-teak unit, designed by architect S. K. Sheldon, of Cambridge, Massachusetts, and built by Michael Standish, of Jamaica Plain, Massachusetts, came about. Solid teak boards make up the counter and backsplash; teak veneer covers the curved apron, case side, and door. Standish made the curved pieces by gluing up two layers of ⅜-in. bendable plywood around a form and then gluing on a cloth-backed teak veneer. Because both bathroom walls were somewhat out of plumb, he left the ends of the case and apron long, scribing them to fit during installation. (For more on scribing, see pp.44-45.) Photo by Sandor Nagyszalanczy.

Bathroom Built-in Storage

People store a lot of stuff in bathrooms: toiletries and makeup supplies, paper goods, cleansers, and towels. The typical sink vanity can rarely hold everything—especially in a full bath. The challenge for the designer/builder is to create built-in units that impinge minimally upon the limited floor space yet provide maximum storage capacity.

In the bathroom shown in the photo at left, John Marckworth, of Port Townsend, Washington, designed and built an alcove of cabinetry around the freestanding pedestal sink. To the left of the sink, a bifold door encloses storage shelves; the unit to the right of the sink hides a plumbing stack that could not be moved. Note the eye-comforting carry-over of the shadow lines of the drawers through the backsplash and to the right-hand unit. To provide access to a clean-out, Marckworth attached the bottom panel of the unit on the right with two-part touch-fastener strips.

During the course of an extensive remodel, unusual opportunities may arise to stimulate some unique and creative solutions for built-in storage. To take advantage of the 40-in.-deep under-stairway space that appeared as an extensive remodel opened up a bathroom, woodworker Tom Phillips, of Ashland, Oregon, decided to fill the space completely with storage fixtures (see the photo on the facing page). He realized that the top line of drawers and cubbies would have a stepped look, but instead of hiding the existence of the stairs, he decided instead to draw attention to them. Oak "treads" contrast with madrone "risers" while 1½-in. by 2-in. oak "balusters" (pinned into the treads at the bottom and lag-bolted to the wall framing at the top) provide

Floor-to-ceiling, multipurpose cabinets by John Marckworth provide efficient and versatile storage by the sink. Photo by Craig Wester.

Taking both aesthetic and functional advantage of a stairway temporarily exposed during a remodel, these cubbies and drawers by Tom Phillips appear to march up the end wall of the bathroom. The materials and styling match the sink vanity. Photo by Robert Jaffe.

nailing for the ¾-in. mahogany-plywood wall partition. Phillips formed the interior partitions of the under-stair units with ¾-in. plywood to provide surfaces for drawer slides and to create walls for the cupboard areas.

In the photo at left, an innovative little cupboard is tucked into the corner of a small bathroom. Because the unit rotates on lazy Susan hardware (each module independently), the shelving can be kept shallow, so medicine bottles and other small articles are easy to see and reach. (For these items, a deep cabinet would almost be a waste of space.) The unit was designed and built by Keith Evans (Zoom Corporation) of Canonsburg, Pennsylvania.

For storage that doesn't call attention to itself, see the photo below. The medicines and toiletries in this bathroom are stashed in cubbies

To get into these medicine cabinets by Keith Evans, one simply gives them a push—they rotate to the open position. Photo by Stephen Burchesky.

The space between wall studs gave Tom Bosworth the opportunity to create a series of enclosed cubbies for medicine and toiletries. Photo by Craig Wester.

constructed between the wall studs. Self-closing, hidden cup hinges allow the close-fitting doors to be adjusted to an even margin line. A removable sheet of plastic laminate on the floor of each cubby makes cleaning quick and easy. The cabinetry was designed by architect Tom Bosworth, of Seattle, Washington, and built by Ravenhill Construction, of Friday Harbor, Washington.

The bathroom shown in the photos at right presented a challenge: Create tasteful and useful shelving with minimalist styling, both in the choice of materials and in the shelving's support system. At the same time, the shelves had to be attached securely to the wall—which in this bathroom meant the smooth concrete wall of a former pump house. The designer's solution: have the builder drill holes through the length of a 1¼-in. square fir block and then slip it over a lag bolt (with its head sawn off) anchored in the concrete (see the drawing at right). The ½-in.-thick sandblasted shelves were then spot-glued with clear construction adhesive to the support blocks to prevent slippage. The shelving was designed by architect Geoffrey Prentiss, of Seattle, Washington, and built by Giovanni Giustina, of Friday Harbor, Washington.

Glass shelves designed by Geoffrey Prentiss provide simple, uncluttered storage in a bathroom with concrete walls. Photos by Craig Wester.

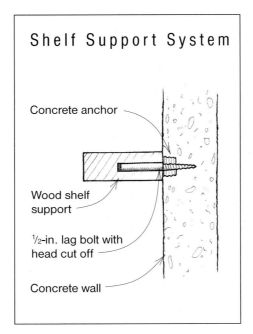

Shelf Support System

Concrete anchor

Wood shelf support

½-in. lag bolt with head cut off

Concrete wall

Closet Built-ins

Built-ins offer closet storage solutions in two basic ways: They can create a closet where none existed, or they can provide a storage system within an existing closet to make the best use of its space. In the photos below and on the facing page you see an extreme—and exceptional—illustration of the latter. Here, a massive, 14-ft.-long furnishing forms a wall-to-wall run of hanging closets that flank a mirrored dressing area. Hinged doors can close off the area when it's not being used.

The built-in bureau features two banks of roomy drawers and a marble counter surface. Above the counter, smaller drawers hold jewelry just below eye level, while cubbies offer additional storage up to the ceiling of the unit. If you look carefully, you may notice that the drawer faces curve inward and the top shelves curve outward as they approach the ceiling—design strategies that create a comfortable sense of

Phillipus Sollman's massive combination wardrobe closet and dressing room, which fills an entire wall of a bedroom, is actually one built-in furnishing. Photo by Phillipus Sollman.

enclosure around the person getting dressed. The soffit—positioned to tie in with the window curtain-rod banding that flows around the perimeter of the room—contains downlighting (placed directly over the waney edge of the veneer) to show off the dramatic figure of the locally cut cherry veneer on the doors. A second soffit hung on the back of the doors provides downlighting on the mirrors. These lights turn on automatically when the dressing-room doors are opened.

Sollman's dressing area can be hidden behind hinged doors (above). At left, the bureau and the center of the furnishing feature subtle curves, a marble counter, and artful lighting. Photos by Phillipus Sollman.

The built-in bed furnishing of shop-made hard maple veneer over medium-density fiberboard (MDF) shown in the photos and drawing below and on the facing page forms one entire wall of a master bedroom while creating closet storage for a child's bedroom on its opposite side. Directly behind the headboard is a cubby space with adjustable shelving for storage. Pegs set in a line below the cubby are for everyday clothes that don't need hangers, such as work pants and sweatshirts—the garments are easy to see and to grab, and at a height kids can reach. The unit was designed by Weinstein Copeland Architects, of Seattle, Washington, and built by Bill Walker, also of Seattle.

Who says a wardrobe unit must always be placed either against a wall or into a recess? Certainly not architect

The casework of this built-in, designed by Weinstein Copeland Architects, creates a wall that provides bedroom furnishings for a master bedroom on one side (above) and a closet storage system for a child's room on the other (facing page). Photo by Craig Wester.

Section through Bed Platform and Wall

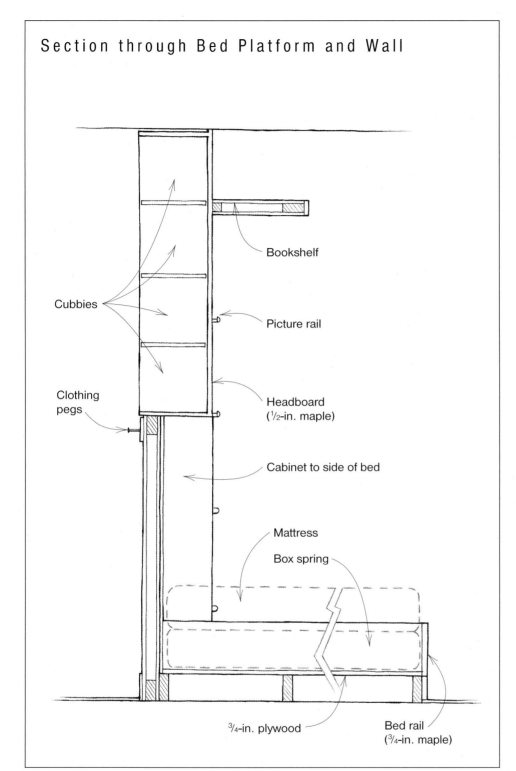

Cubbies

Clothing pegs

Bookshelf

Picture rail

Headboard ($\frac{1}{2}$-in. maple)

Cabinet to side of bed

Mattress

Box spring

$\frac{3}{4}$-in. plywood

Bed rail ($\frac{3}{4}$-in. maple)

Open cubbies and pegs make a convenient "closet" for a child's bedroom. Photo by Jim Tolpin.

Alan Liddle's free-standing wardrobe/bookcase for a master bedroom stores both clothing and books and also acts as a room screen. The roll-down fabric "doors" of the closet match the room's window screens. Photo by Craig Wester.

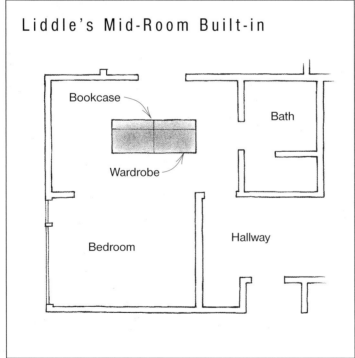

Liddle's Mid-Room Built-in

Bookcase

Bath

Wardrobe

Bedroom

Hallway

Alan Liddle, of Tacoma, Washington. Instead Liddle placed a floor-to-ceiling unit away from all the walls of a home's single bedroom (see the photo above). This unusual situation allowed the furnishing to function as a hanging wardrobe and closet storage on the side facing the bed and a bookcase on the opposite side (see the drawing at left). The unit also acts as a screen in front of the bedroom's broad hallway—allowing the bedroom to remain open for light and ventilation to the rest of the home.

The bowed front, curved plinth, and unusual brass pulls of the built-in dresser shown in the photo below right lend much elegance to what might otherwise have been a rather bland wardrobe closet with built-in drawers. Notice how the side walls of the dresser extend to the closet's ceiling to provide support for closet rods (stacked one above the other) and a hat shelf. Another unusual feature of this closet is the slide-out shoe rack (see the photo below left), which is mounted on full-extension slides. A light pull from your toe brings the rack out from beneath the hanging clothes and into the light. This innovative built-in accessory keep shoes organized and out of the way, yet they're exceptionally easy to get at when needed. The dresser was designed and built by Dean Coley, of Watsonville, California.

Dean Coley's elegant built-in quartersawn red oak dresser, close to furniture in design and execution, graces a wardrobe closet. To the right of the dresser is a clever slide-out shoe rack. Photos by Sandor Nagyszalanczy.

The closet storage fixture shown in the photo below is composed of casework and shelf modules—though here the deep cubicles toward the bottom are fitted with drawer boxes. Unlike shelves, drawers bring their contents out into the space and light of a room, making their contents much easier to access. To maximize the space in the closet (which was the only closet in a 625-sq.-ft. home), the designer and builder, Charley Ingle, of Sopchoppy, Florida, did something really clever: He stepped out the drawer cubicles to form steps, providing access to the upper shelves. This "stepstool" allowed him to place the shelves well above normal height, taking full advantage of the room's 10-ft. ceiling. The drawing below shows the overall dimensions of the storage systems.

Dumbwaiters

Dumbwaiters, either motorized or manually operated, are a useful and increasing popular built-in furnishing,

Drawer units by Charley Ingle step out, creating a "stepstool" that provides access to high storage shelves. Photo by Joe Witt.

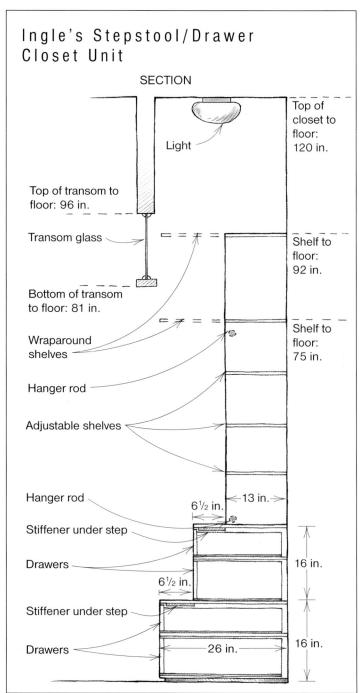

Ingle's Stepstool/Drawer Closet Unit

SECTION

Light

Top of closet to floor: 120 in.

Top of transom to floor: 96 in.

Transom glass

Shelf to floor: 92 in.

Bottom of transom to floor: 81 in.

Wraparound shelves

Shelf to floor: 75 in.

Hanger rod

Adjustable shelves

Hanger rod

13 in.

6½ in.

Stiffener under step

Drawers

16 in.

6½ in.

Stiffener under step

16 in.

Drawers

26 in.

especially in homes with two or more stories. The dumbwaiter—which looks like a built-in wall cupboard when closed—is most commonly used in homes for bringing up groceries from the garage to the kitchen or for hauling firewood up from the basement to a fireplace.

For safety, nearly all dumbwaiters feature an automatic brake should the cable(s) break. More sophisticated motorized versions offer additional safety features—the unit won't operate if any doors are open, and doors cannot be opened unless the cab is at that floor level—an important safety feature to consider if children or pets are in the household. The cab itself usually has a drop-down or fold-out door panel to contain and prevent shifting of the contents during the lift.

Dumbwaiters are available in a range of load capacities—most fall between 65 lb. to 500 lb. Of course, the higher the rating, the more expensive the unit (from $800 to $8,000, not including shaft construction). To save money, some brands offer hardware kits—you build

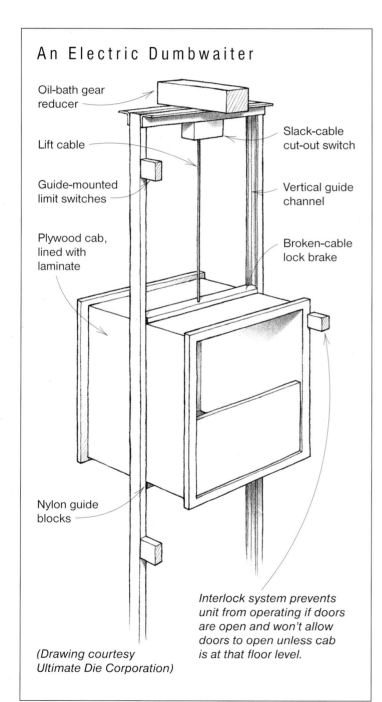

An Electric Dumbwaiter

Oil-bath gear reducer

Lift cable

Guide-mounted limit switches

Plywood cab, lined with laminate

Nylon guide blocks

Slack-cable cut-out switch

Vertical guide channel

Broken-cable lock brake

Interlock system prevents unit from operating if doors are open and won't allow doors to open unless cab is at that floor level.

(Drawing courtesy Ultimate Die Corporation)

A common and eminently useful location for a dumbwaiter is near a fireplace, where it serves to bring wood up from a lower floor. Photo courtesy Miller Manufacturing.

the cab yourself from plywood and other materials. Checking local codes for shaft-way construction specifications is a must, since many communities require the use of a fire-rated drywall lining. In some areas, codes require the dumb-waiter to be installed by a factory representative or elevator subcontractor.

Laundry Centers

Built-in furnishings can be used to create and define a laundry center in a home, either as a part of a kitchen or within a dedicated room. Architect Dick Reed, of Portland, Maine, created a laundry center by placing built-in cabinets in the

A hide-away laundry by Dick Reed flanks a passageway: on one side, a cabinet with a built-in ironing board, on the other, a closet for the washer and dryer. Photo © Brian Vanden Brink.

passageway between the kitchen and a living area (see the photo on the facing page). In use, the space becomes a laundry room; when not needed, the laundry equipment completely disappears. To hide the presence of the door, the cabinetmaker hung it with Soss "invisible" hinges. Notice how the closet door jogs at an angle to accommodate the wall layout. The cabinets were built by Walter Crandell, of Peaks Island, Maine.

In the second example, designer Ed Charest, of Ellicott City, Maryland, set stacking washer and dryer units into a full-height corner cabinet—when the machines are out of use, they can disappear behind a pair of flipper doors (see the top photo at right). Wall cabinets to either side contain detergent and other laundry products; pull-out wire hampers are handy for sorting laundry by color and fabric. A peninsula counter separates the laundry area from the kitchen and makes a convenient surface for folding clothes, towels, and sheets.

The cabinetry in the third example, designed by Weinstein Copeland Architects, of Seattle Washington, and built by Bill Walker, also of Seattle, doesn't even look like a laundry at first glance (see the bottom photo at right). A closer look will reveal the large roll-out hampers under the counter surface. When filled with clothes, they can be pulled over to the stacked washer and dryer in the closet at the end of the hall. The upper cabinets hold laundry supplies, while the valance between them contains downlighting. Clothes can be sorted and folded on the plastic-laminate counter or hung on the closet pole.

This laundry center by Ed Charest features pull-out wire hampers and a flipper-door washer/dryer closet. Photo courtesy Maytag Appliance.

Efficiently placed and cleanly designed laundry-room cabinets and roll-out hampers by Weinstein Copeland Architects fill one wall of a hallway leading to the washer and dryer. Photo by Craig Wester.

Two Wine Cellars

The wine cellar can certainly be a challenge to the cabinetmaker, who must figure out how to design and build a furnishing that can store hundreds of bottles in an efficient and aesthetically pleasing way. In the example shown in the photo below, designer and builder J. Scott Publicover, of Boise, Idaho, set floor-to-ceiling racks of solid redwood along two walls of a stone-lined cellar. Each vertical 4-in.-wide rack section holds up to 12 bottles of wine. Because this is the number of bottles in a standard case, the layout of the rack makes it easy to catalog and map the wine cellar's holdings.

Certain styling elements are effective as well: A brass inlay glued to the faces of the two horizontal trim bands creates an elegant visual boundary, breaking up what might otherwise have been a rather monotonous geometric pattern. On the third wall of the room next to the staircase, there's a wine-tasting alcove with cupboards for glassware and a small refrigerator. The trim of the alcove extends around the door, tying this area in with the rest of the wine cellar.

Redwood racks by J. Scott Publicover hold up to 600 bottles of wine in a stone-lined basement wine cellar. Photo by J. Scott Publicover.

Instead of building wine racks into the walls of an existing space, builder Del Cover, of San Diego, California, created a wine cellar of solid walnut and glass within an elegant basement office (see the photo below). The wine cellar encloses and hides the underside of a stairway that passes through the wall of the office on the way to another part of the basement (if you look closely, you can detect the angled ceiling through the glass doors). Cover took advantage of the side walls of the wine cellar to build in adjustable-shelf bookcases.

Massive fluted columns that appear to support the heavy floor beams make the wine cellar seem integral to the architecture of the room. The carved corbels further emphasize the columns' apparent structural relevance.

A solid-walnut wine cellar by Del Cover hides the underside of a stairway in a basement office. Photo by Del Cover.

11
BEDROOMS

A bed is a bed—a place to lie down. But as a built-in furnishing, as an integral component of a home's interior landscape, a bed can become much more than that: It can nestle into an intimate, cozy space within, yet separate from, the bustling activity in the rest of the house.

Scandinavian interior architecture, which inspired the design of the Maine island home shown in the photo on the facing page, typically calls for beds to be built into an alcove. Not only does the resulting sleeping space look cozy and inviting—it is. The walls and partitions that surround the bed block chilly drafts and trap body-generated heat. At the same time, the alcove bedroom (especially if it has built-in storage for clothing and bedding) maximizes the use of floor space. This, of course, allows the house to be built smaller, making it more economical to construct and to heat.

Scandinavian-style built-in bedroom beds create a delightfully warm and cozy sleeping space in a turn-of-the-century island retreat in Maine. Designer and builder unknown. Photo © Brian Vanden Brink.

A cross between a bed and a cabinet, Duane Paluska's furnishing stands within a showroom
for antiques. Photo © Brian Vanden Brink.

An Enclosure, an Angle, and a Loft

"Make my bed appear as an architectural/furniture statement" was the client's design imperative. Taking inspiration from the bedroom furnishings of Northern Europe (as well as the styling elements of the Orient), woodworker Duane Paluska, of Brunswick, Maine, created a bedroom for a client whose sleeping space had to double as a showroom for antiques.

Built like a huge cabinet, the furnishing (see the photo on the facing page) encloses a queen-sized bed behind cherry-wood slats joined at hard-maple posts. Access to the bed is through doors that slide in grooves cut into the maple framework. Inside, cubbies hold clocks, lamps, and nighttime reading, while large drawers for bedding slide out from under the bed (they ride on slide hardware mounted to the vertical support partitions). The handles and spring-loaded catches are solid ebony. When the doors are slid shut, soft light filters inside through the door's "louvers" (made from dowels) and between the gapped spruce boards that form the "ceiling."

Because the cherry boards that form the side panels can change dimension over time, Paluska joined the boards with tongues and grooves—a strategy that keeps their faces even while allowing the individual boards to shrink and expand across their width with changes in humidity (see the drawing below). Moldings sandwich the ends of the boards where they meet the posts— another strategy that allows them free movement while maintaining alignment.

Here's a challenge: how do you create a bedroom in a tiny, odd-shaped house without sacrificing its sense of openness and free flow of light and air? The

Paluska's Floating Slats

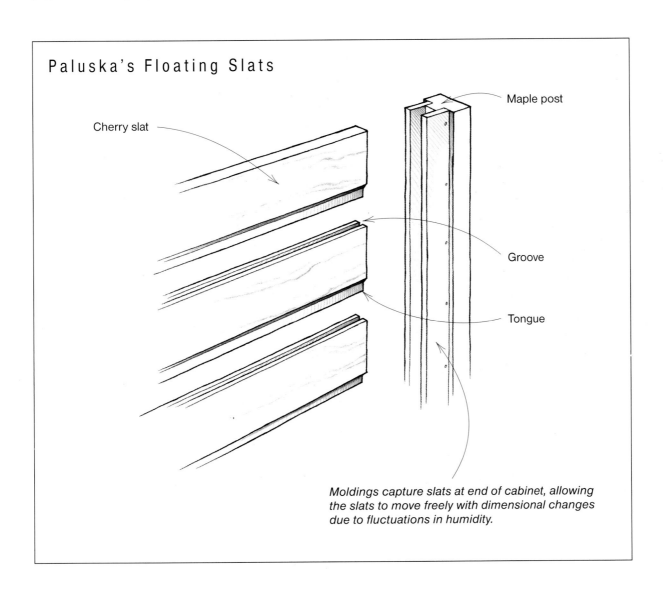

Cherry slat

Maple post

Groove

Tongue

Moldings capture slats at end of cabinet, allowing the slats to move freely with dimensional changes due to fluctuations in humidity.

The "bedroom" of this tiny house is a raised-bed platform and attendant cabinetry designed by
Geoffrey Prentiss. Photo by Craig Wester.

solution offered by architect Geoffrey Prentiss, of Seattle, Washington, was to eliminate the bedroom as a separate space and instead provide a thoughtful construction of built-in furnishings to serve as a sleeping area (see the photo on the facing page).

With angles recalling the footprint of the house (see the drawing below), clear, vertical-grain fir plywood casework with pine plywood facings forms a bed platform, a headboard with storage, and an upper cabinet with glass doors. The fir plywood casework is joined at the corners with splined miters. To absorb abrasion and prevent subsequent splintering, the exposed mitered edges are replaced with a strip of solid fir. Side cupboards provide additional storage for clothes and bedding. The furnishing was built by Giovanni Giustina, under contractor Peter Kilpatrick (Ravenhill Construction) of Friday Harbor, Washington.

An Angled Bed in an Angular House

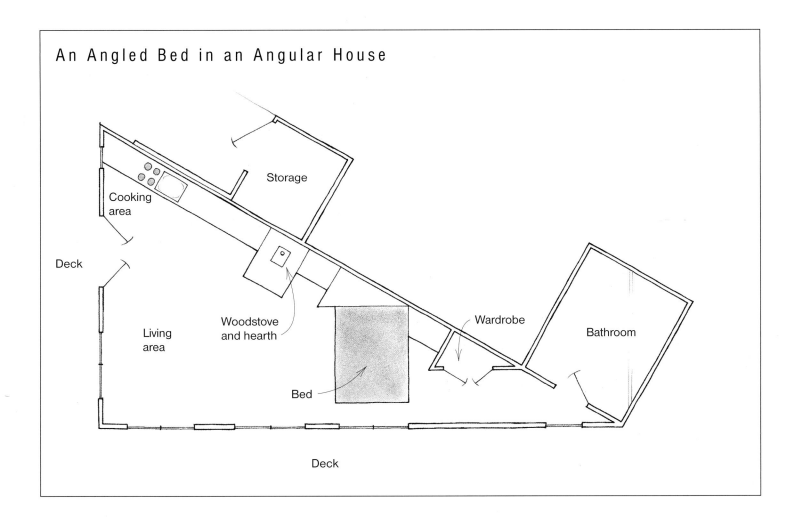

Storage

Cooking area

Deck

Living area

Woodstove and hearth

Bed

Wardrobe

Bathroom

Deck

Architect Paul Duncker, of Jackson, Wyoming, went a step further (literally a number of steps) than Prentiss to deal with a small living space. Taking advantage of a 13-ft.-high ceiling, Duncker designed and built a 7-ft.-high stairway and storage system that also supports a sleeping loft (see the photo below left) in the living room of a small apartment. The unit, built of red oak, dramatically increases the home's usable floor space and also provides innovative storage—from an entertainment center to a lighted art display alcove to a mini-wine cellar (see the drawing on the facing page).

To ensure that the casework would be strong enough to support the weight of a second floor, Duncker constructed the 3-in.-thick walls of the unit by sandwiching ¾-in. oak plywood around 2x4 studs. Because the unit covers a run of baseboard heating units, each riser is pierced with a small aperture to vent out the rising heat (see the photo below right). The design is clever, but be aware that drawers and cupboard doors built into stairs—as well as the unusually high risers of this unit and the lack of guard rails along the loft—will probably not meet building codes in most areas of the country.

This built-in by Paul Duncker supports a sleeping loft and provides a variety of storage solutions for a small, high-ceiling apartment. Vents in the stair steps allow heat to rise. Photos by Paul Duncker.

Duncker's Stair Cabinet and Loft

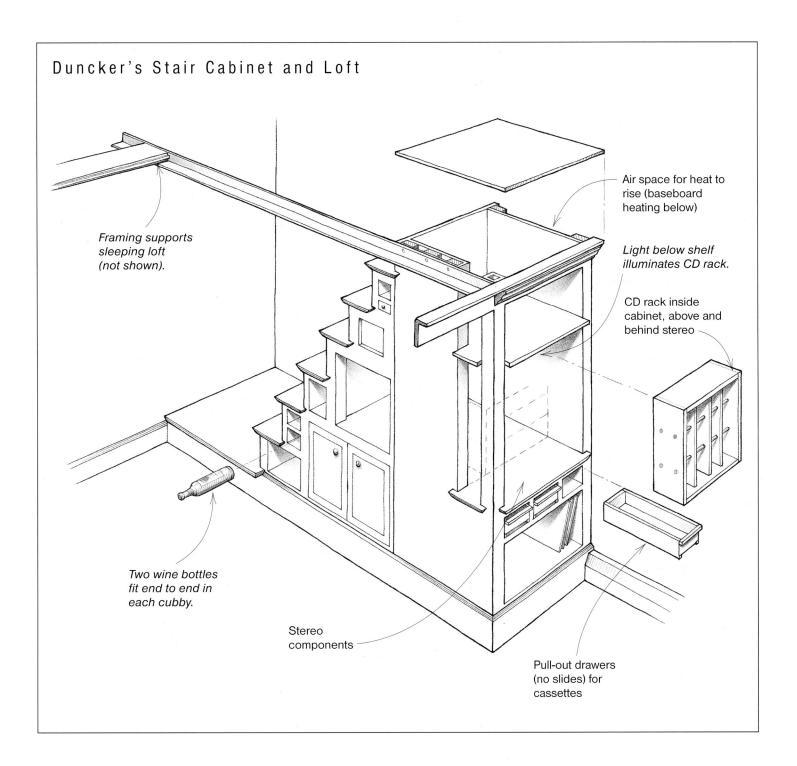

Framing supports sleeping loft (not shown).

Air space for heat to rise (baseboard heating below)

Light below shelf illuminates CD rack.

CD rack inside cabinet, above and behind stereo

Two wine bottles fit end to end in each cubby.

Stereo components

Pull-out drawers (no slides) for cassettes

The Bedroom Suite

Thoughtfully designed and well-crafted built-in furnishings lend functional beauty to a bedroom, as in the suite shown in the photo below. Here, a client's desire for a tranquil, Japanese-style interior inspired woodworker Cliff Nathan, of Studio City, California, to design and build a bedroom suite of casework, shelving, and *shoji* doors.

To evoke a feeling of Oriental serenity, Nathan chose light-colored, low-figured hard maple to create cabinets with crisp lines (note the lack of moldings) and simple proportional relationships. He built the cases of ¾-in. maple plywood, using solid maple for the drawer faces and walnut veneer in the horizontal reveal line. Because the counter surface of one of the side units was greater than 8 ft.—the greatest available length of

A suite of built-in maple furnishings by Cliff Nathan brings a Japanese-style ambience to a bedroom. Photo by Kay Donohew.

maple-faced plywood—Nathan decided to make the tops by applying a veneer of hard maple to a plywood substrate. He made the drawers out of Baltic birch and mounted them on full-extension slides. To allow the dresser to stand free of the floor, he lag-bolted the unit securely to the wall studs.

To reduce the protrusion of the television into the room, Nathan created a recess by cutting a hole through the bedroom wall and into an adjoining wardrobe closet (see the photo below). A 2x4 "sill" installed across the wall studs supports for the one-piece unit, which consists of the television surround and the shelves that extend out to either side.

Called in to renovate a dark cubicle that passed as a master bedroom, designer and builder Gary Milici, of Seattle, Washington, turned to built-in furnishings and a sunroom addition to

The television surround and a shelf, supported by a recess cut into the adjoining closet, appear to be suspended on the wall. Photo by Kay Donohew.

In this bedroom, remodeled by Gary Milici, an angled corner cabinet for television equipment, artwork, and linens (right) faces a bed, set at the same angle, in the opposite corner (below). Photos by W. Stephen Holding.

breathe new life into the room. To create space for a furnishing that would contain a television and a linen closet (see the photo at top left), Milici tore out an existing hallway. Angling the unit across the newly framed room corner oriented the television toward the bed, and, as a side benefit, created triangular spaces that were perfect for art display shelves (each shelf is illuminated with strip lighting). A new linen closet placed behind the unit can be reached from a hallway that runs along the outside of the bedroom.

In the opposite corner of the bedroom, Milici built in a headboard (note the matching soffit, which houses downlighting) and a bay window filled with book shelving (see the photo at bottom left). The headboard angles the bed to face the new sunroom addition and the corner cabinet.

Bedrooms for Kids

Unlike the rest of us (except for Sunday mornings), children live in their bedrooms. Here they spend hours sleeping, dreaming, and playing. For children who sleep on an ordinary cot, the bed is not so special. For children who are fortunate enough to have been given a furnishing designed with a child's life in mind, the bed can be the most memorable piece of furniture they will ever own.

It's not likely that any child could forget this playhouse/bed space shown in the photos on the facing page, which was designed by architect Steven Foote in response to his 10-year-old daughter's concept of what a bedroom (and a house) should be. Foote, of Boston, Massachusetts, framed an alcove 4 ft. deep by 6 ft. long into the end wall of a

The child's ultimate fantasy bedroom—a doll-house come to life—was designed by Steven Foote and his daughter Caroline. Photos © Brian Vanden Brink.

stair landing—a space just large enough to contain a child-size futon. A circular window, which can be opened, provides natural light and ventilation. The angled "pathway" is an illusion created with angles and color contrasts—it is in reality a vertical ladder with oak treads and "flower stamens" to serve as handholds. Find the handle for the door—hint: look closely at the "tree."

When Carol Hasse, of Port Townsend, Washington, designed her bedroom, she knew she wanted it to feature a large window seat—yet she also wanted a nursery. The thought occurred that they could be one and the same—at least until the baby grew up and out of the bedroom. Hasse, a sailmaker by trade, had her custom-made nylon netting installed at the front and back of the alcove (see the photo below). The netting allows plenty of light and air to pass through, yet safely contains an active baby. The drawers below the seat are for bedding. The window seat was built by Alex Spear, also of Port Townsend.

Builder Greg Wallace, of Redding, Connecticut, thought that a window seat would be a perfect addition to his child's bedroom (see the photo on the facing page). The seat would be a quiet contemplative alcove, an ideal place to sit and read with a child. Underneath, he

Carol Hasse's large window seat, outfitted with soft nylon netting, serves temporarily as a crib. Photo by Craig Wester.

incorporated a toy box, whose lid supports the seat cushions. On one side, open shelving holds playthings and stuffed animals; on the other a closet-like storage cabinet contains clothing and diapers. To keep the seat toasty warm, Wallace ran a baseboard heat loop under the furnishing and vented it so air could circulate around (see the drawing below).

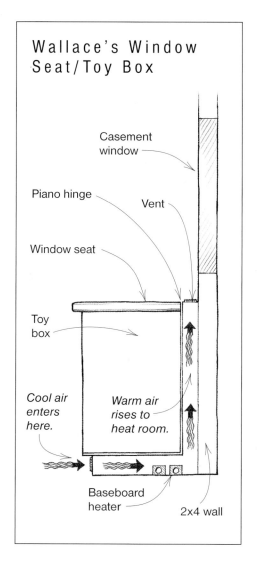

Wallace's Window Seat/Toy Box

Casement window

Piano hinge

Vent

Window seat

Toy box

Cool air enters here.

Warm air rises to heat room.

Baseboard heater

2x4 wall

Greg Wallace made use of natural light, a baseboard heater, and softwood tones and textures to create a cozy sitting area in a child's bedroom. Photo by Sloan T. Howard Photography.

Murphy Beds

A bedroom does not have to have a bed that shows all the time. Named after William L. Murphy, the American inventor who developed the hardware in the early 1920s after falling asleep standing up (just kidding!), the Murphy bed disappears in seconds into a cabinet or closet. With the bed hidden, a bedroom gets a lot larger, making the room available for other activities besides sleeping—a significant advantage in small homes.

Taking advantage of Murphy-style hardware (see the sidebar on the facing page), woodworker Dennis Slabaugh, of Naples, Florida, designed and built a wall-to-wall unit that combines space for a computer and printer, books, and two lateral legal-size file drawers with a guest bed in the family's multipurpose room (see the photos at left). With the bed out of the way, the room converts to an office and an exercise space. To make installation easier, Slabaugh built the biscuit-joined ³⁄₄-in. birch plywood unit in five sections: the desk with side cabinet, the side cupboard with file drawers, the two upper shelf units, and the header that connects the units to either side of the bed. The finish is white-tinted, water-based polyurethane.

When Dennis Slabaugh's Murphy bed folds up into the wall, this bedroom becomes an office and an exercise room. Photos by Dennis Slabaugh.

Spring-type hinge and counterweight systems for Murphy beds are typically mounted on a board and anchored to the floor behind the bed's headboard—the hardware is hidden whether the bed is open or closed. Spring systems (see the photo at top right) are easy to operate and offer almost no resistance when you raise or lower the bed. A screw mechanism on the spring canister lets you adjust the spring to the weight of your particular bed and bedding.

Pneumatic, or piston, systems (see the illustration at bottom right) mount between the cabinet and the bed rather than to the floor. In this location the hardware is visible when the bed is open, but there is less chance of misalignment developing between the bed frame and the surrounding casework. Like the spring system, the piston system does most of the work for you—less than 20 lb. of force is required to lift a bed.

Both spring and piston systems can be mounted to lift the bed vertically or horizontally. For safety—as well as for smooth operation, it is critical to follow the hardware manufacturer's specifications and installation instructions.

The Sico spring system. Photo courtesy Sico.

The Hafele Pneumatic Piston System

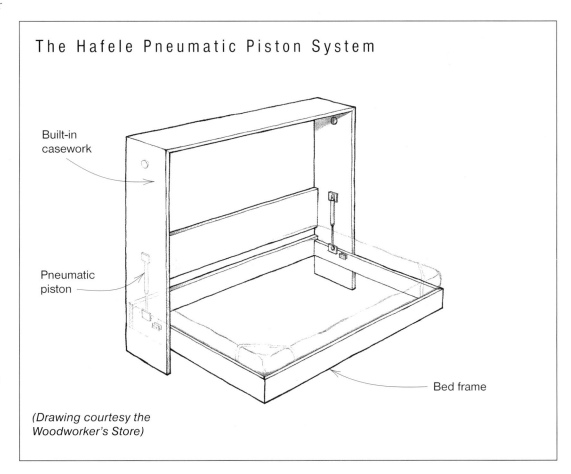

Built-in casework

Pneumatic piston

Bed frame

(Drawing courtesy the Woodworker's Store)

Headboards

A built-in headboard can contribute much to the interior architecture of a home—far more than a couple of boards tacked unceremoniously to the end of a bed. As a built-in furnishing, the headboard anchors the bed, both literally and aesthetically, to the style and structure of the room.

On a more modern note than the Yaddo Mansion headboard shown in the photo below is the piece shown in the photo on the facing page. Built of painted poplar, this built-in bed furnishing with side tables melds with a latticed wall opening. The gabled headboard, designed by architect John

Dwarfed by its wall-to-wall headboard, the bed looks insignificant. What dreams one might have beneath these neo-Gothic ramparts! Designed by 19th-century architect William Halsey Wood and original owner Katrina Trask for her home, Yaddo Mansion, built in Saratoga Springs, N.Y., in 1893. Photo © Brian Vanden Brink.

Silverio, of Lincolnville, Maine, and Floss Barber, of Philadelphia, Pennsylvania, is similar in intent to the massive, house-like moldings of the Yaddo Mansion (though it is certainly much more restrained). In both, the woodworking is distinctly architectural, relating the bed furnishing to the style and structure of the home itself. On an emotional level, both architectural furnishings create feelings of security and coziness—of snuggling under the protective roof of a home. In the modern piece, the gable with latticed circle mimics the front of the house—which happens to form one wall of this bedroom. The latticed wall opening provides cross ventilation and gives the bedroom a feeling of openness.

A gabled headboard by John Silverio and Floss Barber incorporates a latticed opening to create sight lines and ventilation to an adjoining dressing room. Photo © Brian Vanden Brink.

Peter Bohlin's head-board of intertwined birch branches isn't just built-in—it looks to be "grown in." Photo © Brian Vanden Brink.

In the bedroom of a mountain retreat deep in the Adirondack Mountains, a headboard made of birch saplings extends its branches up from the bed and into the upper reaches of the room to entwine with the log collar ties (see the photo on the facing page). Designed by architect Peter Bohlin, of Pittsburgh, Pennsylvania, and built by Ken Heitz, of Indian Lake, New York, the headboard reflects and builds upon the ambience of the home. The side tables, the built-in bench at the foot of the bed, and the table lamps are all made of rustic materials.

Designer and builder Steve Saxe, of Vail, Colorado, recessed an arch of knotty pine veneer plywood into a framed alcove to create a cozy embrace around the head of a bed (see the photo below). Within the arch, cubbies form "night tables" to either side of the bed. Next to the bed, a solid pine door— its top cut arched to the same radius as the headboard recess—opens into a storage area behind the bed.

To get the 1/4-in. bias-ply knotty pine plywood to conform to the considerable bend of the arch, Saxe framed up a bending brake of 2x4 and 2x2s.

(Bending plywood would have bent more easily, but was not readily available in pine.) Saxe began the bending process by moistening the outer plies of the plywood and then setting the panel out in the sun to warm up—this helped the fibers become more pliable and thus more amenable to bending. The first day, Saxe bent the panel to fit between the outermost cleats. Each succeeding day, after another treatment of moisture and sun, he moved the panel in a notch, gradually increasing the radius of the bend.

Steve Saxe's recessed headboard was formed with an arch of pine plywood. Photo by Steve Saxe.

EPILOG

We have now seen how built-in furnishings can find a place in nearly every room of a house, from the living room to the bedroom. Some units, such as entertainment centers, are necessarily massive and complex. Others, like South Mountain Co.'s "night table," shown in the photo on the facing page, are incredibly simple. Barely a built-in, but a built-in nonetheless, it was created by setting a board into a recess framed by the head of a bed. Straightforward, effective, opportunistic, and aesthetically satisfying—it is all that a built-in should be.

Whether simple or complex, furnishings that creatively and artfully blend furniture with architecture can contribute style, function, and even magic to our everyday living spaces. It is as hard to imagine a home that could not benefit from built-ins as it is to imagine living in a home without them.

Photo by Derrill Bazzy.

CONTRIBUTORS

Albrecht, Peter
P.O. Box 5506
Port Townsend, WA 98368

Alexander, Rex
12653 Griffith Rd.
Brethren, MI 49619

Arentz, Joseph
10 Bunker Hill Rd.
Stevens, PA 17578

Beers, Christopher
307 Lakeside Dr.
Ramsey, NJ 07446

Benson, Roger
5 Merriam Way
Upton, MA 01568

Bethanis, Peter
Bethanis Associates, Inc.
P.O. Box 283
Kents Hill, ME 04349

Bohlin, Peter
Bohlin Cywinski Jackson
307 4th Ave.
Suite 1300
Pittsburgh, PA 15222

Bosworth, Tom
4532 E. Laurel Dr. NE
Seattle, WA 98105

Brackett, Len
East Wind, Inc.
21020 Shields Camp Rd.
Nevada City, CA 95959

Bringham, Jim
Woodstuff Custom
   Woodworking
5405 Oben Fell Court
Antelope, CA 95843

Cabitt, Stephen
Stephen M. Cabitt Co.
55 Glen St.
Rowley, MA 01969

Capps, Bill
KooserRun Design
RD 6, Box 313
Somerset, PA 15501

Centerbrook Architects
(James C. Childress,
   Mariette Hines Gomez,
   Jefferson Riley, Mark
   Simon)
Box 955
Essex, CT 06426

Chan, Lo-Yi
270 Riverside Dr.
New York, NY 10025

Chapin, Ross
Ross Chapin and Associates
Box 230
Langley, WA 98260

Charest, Ed
Specialty Trim Co.
12322 Benson Branch Rd.
Ellicott City, MD 21042

Cheng, Lawrence
39 Crescent St.
Cambridge, MA 02138

Coley, Dean
Architectural Millwork and
   Design
P.O. Box 2110
Watsonville, CA 95077

Cover, Del
4902 Gaylord Dr.
San Diego, CA 92117

Day, Ross
Ross Day Fine Furniture
3134 Elliott Ave. #220
Seattle, WA 98121

Duncker, Paul
P.O. Box 2519
Jackson, WY 83001

Evans, Keith
Zoom Corporation
127 Adams Ave.
Canonsburg, PA 15317

Ferguson, Elaine
860 S. La Luna Ave.
Ojai, CA 93023

Foote, Steven
Perry, Dean, Rodgers &
   Partners
177 Milk St.
Boston, MA 02109

Ned Forrest Architects
525 Broadway
Sonoma, CA 95476

Friedlander, Cliff
316 Fairmount Ave.
Santa Cruz, CA 95062

Graham, Barrie
43 Crystal Falls Rd.
Arundel, Quebec J0T 1A0
Canada

Grew-Sheridan, John and
   Carolyn
500 Treat Ave.
San Francisco, CA 94110

Hamilton, Dan and Sheila
P.O. Box 2261
Blufton, SC 29910

Hasse, Carol
6644 Cape George Rd.
Port Townsend, WA 98308

Hermannsson, John
810 Bradford St.
Redwood City, CA 94063

Hoffer, Michael
Rt. 1, Box 381A
Espanola, NM 87532

Ingle, Charley
40 Easy St. S.
Sopchoppy, FL 32358

Irvine, Bill
1980 Cape George Rd.
Port Townsend, WA 98368

Jackson, Dean
Custom Wood Designs
2011 Lawrence Ave. W.
Unit 27
Toronto, Ontario M9N 3V3
Canada

Johnson, Carl
Peninsula Woodworkers
148 Flying Mist Isle
Foster City, CA 94404

Johnson, Neil K.
2800 Route 130, Suite 301
Cinnaminson, NJ 08077

Kagay, Dan
Dan Kagay Fine
   Woodworking
6710 Kings Point W.
Austin, TX 78723

Katz, D. Ralph
Applegate Farm Complex
Cranbury Station Rd.
Cranbury, NJ 08512

Kayner, Alex
P.O. Box 655
Bar Harbor, ME 04609

Kervin, Michael
MGK Construction
267 Seventh Ave. W.
North Bay, Ontario P1B 3P8
Canada

Kilpatrick, Peter
Ravenhill Construction
1800-A Lake Rd.
Friday Harbor, WA 98250

de Klerk, Andrew
536 N. 76th St.
Seattle, WA 98103

Kranzberg, Bruce
BKI, Inc. Commercial
   Woodworking
3210 Valmont, Unit D
Boulder, CO 80301

Langmuir, Jane
107 Bowen St.
Providence, RI 02906

Liddle, Alan
Liddle and Jacklin
703 Pacific Ave.
Tacoma, WA 98402

Mackall, Louis
135 Leetes Island Rd.
Guilford, CT 06437

Marckworth, John
Marckworth Specialty
   Woodworking
536 Cass St.
Port Townsend, WA 98368

Marrs, Galen
311 Jackson
Port Townsend, WA 98368

Matthews, Grady
Grady Matthews Custom
   Cabinetry
23509 29th Ave. W.
Brier, WA 98036

Milici, Gary
Coastline Construction, Inc.
143 NE 61st St.
Seattle, WA 98115

Miller Manufacturing, Inc.
(manual dumbwaiter)
165 Cascade Court
Rohnert Park, CA 94928

Mincey, Richard
Mincey Carpentry
250 McLee Rd.
Lexington, SC 29073

Nathan, Cliff
Cliff Nathan Design
4530 Beeman Ave.
Studio City, CA 91604

Neumann, Andy
888 Linden Ave.
Carpinteria, CA 93013

Nolin, Mike
49 Twin Turn Dr.
Brewster, MA 02631

Nuckols, Paul
Paul Nuckols Fine Carpentry
87 Ingersoll Grove
Springfield, MA 01109

Paluska, Duane
Icon Contemporary Art
19 Mason St.
Brunswick, ME 04011

John Parker
120 Fox Den Rd.
Glastonbury, CT 06033

Pastine, Albert
1183 Shotwell St.
San Francisco, CA 94110

Patterson, Dale
507 Calle De Soto
San Clemente, CA 92672

Paulson, Dan
Paulson Construction
Friday Harbor, WA 98250

Phillips, Tom
Tom Phillips Woodworks
60 Fifth St.
Ashland, OR 97520

Prentiss, Geoffrey
1218 6th Ave. W
Seattle, WA 98119

Price, Jim
642 Overton St.
Newport, KY 41071

Publicover, J. Scott
Scott Publicover
   Construction
8308 W. State St.
Boise, ID 83703

Reed, Dick
Reed & Co. Architecture
30 Pleasant St.
Portland, ME 04101

Saulnier, Ronald
18 Bayard Ave.
Bayville, NY 11709

Saxe, Steve
Custom Craft Carpentry
P.O. Box 5712
Vail, CO 81658

Schupp, Marv
1609 Trossacks Ave.
London, Ontario N5Y 263
Canada

Share, Rick A.
325 Broome St.
New York, NY 10002

Sheldon, S. K.
154 Magazine Street
Cambridge, MA 02139

Sico North America, Inc.
(Murphy-bed hardware)
7525 Cahill Rd.
Minneapolis, MN 55440

Silverio, John
RR1, Box 4725
Lincolnville, ME 04849

Simmons, Tom
214 E. Yanonali St.
Santa Barbara, CA 93101

Slabaugh, Dennis
P.O. Box 9478
Naples, FL 33941

Smelser, Nathaniel
Nathaniel Smelser
   Woodworking
2336 33rd Avenue Dr.
East Bradenton, FL 34208

Smith, Janice
1022 New Jersey St.
Lawrence, KS 66044

Spear, Alex
1916 Willow
Port Townsend, WA 98368

Sollman, Phillipus
318 N. Fillmore Rd.
Bellefonte, PA 16823

South Mountain Co.
P.O. Box 359
Chilmark, MA 02535

Stancioff, Ivan
RR1, Box 4138
Lincolnville, ME 04849

Standish, Michael
160 Williams St.
Jamaica Plain, MA 02130

Sterling, Jim
94 Commercial St.
P.O. Box 7305
Portland, ME 04112

Swartzendruber Hardwood
   Creations
1100 Chicago St.
Goshen, IN 46526

Sylvestre Construction
7708 5th Ave. S.
Minneapolis, MN 55423

Tolpin, Jim
P.O. Box 1933
Port Townsend, WA 98368

Trzcinski, Tom
Kitchen & Bath Concepts
7901 Perry Highway
Pittsburgh, PA 15237

Ultimate Die Corp.
(electric dumbwaiter)
P.O. Box 260306
Tampa, FL 33685

Van Dam, Samuel
Van Dam and Renner,
   Architects
66 West St.
Portland, ME 04102

Vanden Brink, Kathleen
2 Curtis Ave.
Camden, ME 04843

Walker, Bill
10115 NE Kitsap St.
Bainbridge Island, WA 98110

Wallace, Greg
156 Limekiln Rd.
Redding CT 06896

Wedler, Richard
Richard Wedler Cabinetry
11100 Cumpston St. #35
North Hollywood, CA 91601

Weerts, Brian
1726 Shorewood Dr.
St. Anne, IL 60964

Weinstein Copeland
   Architects
121 Stewart St., Suite 200
Seattle, WA 98101

Weisman, David
751 Brooks St.
Ann Arbor, MI 48103

Westrick, Richard and Emily
95 East King St.
Dallastown, PA 17313

Whitten, Rob
Whitten Architects
37 Silver St.
Portland, ME 04112

Williams, Don
6898 Townline Rd.
Williamson, NY 14589

Winchester, Steve
P.O. Box 322
Gilmanton, NH 03237

The Woodworker's Store
(Murphy-bed hardware)
4365 Willow Dr.
Medina, MN 55340

Wynn, Scott
1785 Egbert St.
San Francisco, CA 94124

INDEX

PUBLISHER: James P. Chiavelli

ACQUISITIONS EDITOR: Rick Peters

PUBLISHING COORDINATOR: Joanne Renna

EDITOR: Ruth Dobsevage

LAYOUT ARTIST: Christopher Casey

PRODUCTION MANAGER: Lynne Phillips

ILLUSTRATOR: Michael Gellatly

TYPEFACE: Berling, Nimbus